Purveyors of Change

School Leaders of Color Share Narratives of Student, School, and Community Success

A Volume in Research, Advocacy, Collaboration,
and Empowerment Mentoring Series

Series Editor

Donna Y. Ford
Ohio State University

Research, Advocacy, Collaboration, and Empowerment Mentoring Series

Donna Y. Ford, Series Editor

Purveyors of Change

School Leaders of Color Share Narratives of Student, School, and Community Success

editors

Judy A. Alston
Ashland University

Lawrence Scott
Texas A&M–San Antonio

Sheree N. Alexander
Atlantic City Public Schools

INFORMATION AGE PUBLISHING, INC.
Charlotte, NC • www.infoagepub.com

Library of Congress Cataloging-in-Publication Data

CIP record for this book is available from the Library of Congress
http://www.loc.gov

ISBNs: 978-1-64802-228-9 (Paperback)

978-1-64802-229-6 (Hardcover)

978-1-64802-230-2 (ebook)

Printed in the United States of America

CONTENTS

ACKNOWLEDGMENTS

Judy A. Alston, PhD

As always I am grateful to God for the gift that was deposited into me before my birth which is my ministry of teaching and preaching. Many thanks to my coeditors, Lawrence and Sheree, as well as to each of the contributors, for their patience and their diligence throughout the preparation of this project. This book is also dedicated to the many school leaders as well as professors of color who have been silenced in their careers. We are grateful for the opportunity to dedicate a space and medium for stories to be told by voices often marginalized and unappreciated in the field. And finally, to the one who keeps me grounded and loves me in the midst of it all—my wife, Dr. Cynthia A. Tyson, my comfort, my sounding board, my love, my reality checker, and my perfect puzzle piece.

Lawrence Scott, PhD

First of all, to God be the Glory. Everything I am and ever will be is a direct result of my faith in God and the mission he has commissioned me to complete until my last breath on earth. Much like being an academician, being an administrator has its many challenges and requires a bevy of people that can support you throughout your mission. Although

Purveyors of Change: School Leaders of Color Share Narratives of Student, School, and Community Success, pp. vii–ix

not exhaustive, here is my attempt to thank those who have helped me throughout my mission. Thank you to my coeditors, Dr. Judy Alston and Dr. Sheree Alexander for taking a chance on me for such a project of this magnitude, with intergenerational implications. Thank you to my wife Chiara who allows me to pursue my purpose and constantly reminds me that my role as husband and father are paramount. To my children, Gabriella and Christian, may you continue to build the legacy that was given to me by my parents. I love you both more than you will ever know. I would like to thank my dad who gave me his tenacity and has illustrated to me that anything is possible if you NEVER give up. To my mom who always instills in me the importance of keeping God first and serving others. To my Pastors Keith and Denetrice Graham, who have helped me develop a desire to leave a legacy and provided me and my family a roadmap to ensure spiritual and personal growth. As Pastor Keith always says: "Success is Measured in Succession!"

Thank you to my inner circle of friends who help me walk this walk with fidelity: Brandon Graham, Amir Samandi, Nathan Townsie, Dr. Carey Latimore, and TX State Board of Education Trustee Marisa Perez, and Analco Gonzales. Thank you to my education colleagues who helped me develop as an educational leader: Dr. Sean Kearney, Dr. Elisabeth Krimbill, Dr. Juan Jasso, Dr. Milton Fields, Dr. Mateen Diop, Dr. Willie Black, Dr. Melissa Jozwiak, Dr. Carl Sheparis, Dr. Donna Ford, Provost Lucius Yates, Dr. Ramon Goings, President Cynthia Teniente-Matson, Provost Mike O'Brien, Dr. Ramona Pittman, Dr. Rebekah Piper, Dr. Debbie Vera, Dr. D. Anthony Miles, Darryl Bego, Paula Monroe, and Janelle Mundine. Thank you to my business partners and friends Jake Whittenburg, Ashley Longoria, Mario Ruiz, the Community for Life Foundation Board and Now Word Covenant Church members for helping me find my purpose by helping others find their purpose through community outreach and scholarships. Although this is a first of several book initiatives, I want to encourage everyone who reads this book to reflect on how we can operationalize discussed actionable steps to support educational leaders of color as they continue to be *Purveyors of Change*.

Sheree N. Alexander, EdD

I have learned so many lessons about myself as an educator, an administrator, a mother, a daughter, a wife, a colleague, a friend, and an advocate through the process of birthing this project. I am grateful to God for allowing the season of learning and reflection. To my coeditors Judy, thank you for your unwavering support and mentorship, but most importantly, for your example of leadership. Lawrence, thank you for ensuring these voices are heard! Thank you for your kind spirit! To each contributor, I thank you for sharing your stories and leading so fearlessly. There are warriors out there for our children! To my husband Leon, thank you for always making my heart smile and sharing this life with me. I love you. To my best girl, my Barboo, Mom, thank you for always believing with me! And to my fellow practitioners, we cannot ever stop. If not us, then who?

INTRODUCTION

Words such as *committed, caring, inspiring, vision oriented, intelligent, honest, ethical, confident, difference-maker,* and *transformational,* have been used to describe effective leaders. Navahandi (2006) would suggest that there are four key ingredients to effective leadership: goal achievement, smooth internal processes, group phenomenon, and external adaptability. To simplify a definition, it would be to develop a concerted set of goals, and inspire and influence human capital, and gather resources to operationalize these goals.

Transformational leaders are purveyors of change. A purveyor provides what is needed in their time. Leaders such as Nelson Mandela, Desmond Tutu, Mother Teresa, and Martin Luther King actively created intergenerational change by employing a transformational style of leadership that sought to create a better world. Their fight was to dismantle the tyranny of systematic oppression, inequities, and marginalization. They were purveyors of change.

Similarly, today's P–12 educational leaders who desire to influence positive change are constantly adjusting their leadership style based on the needs of their students, faculty and staff, and community. They provide what is needed in this 21st century school setting. In the case of this volume of chapters, the focus is on those who provide what it needed for leadership, change, and schooling. The bottom line is that effective leadership is the necessary ingredient in achieving educational improvement because "everything rises and falls on leadership" (Maxwell, 1993, p. viii).

Purveyors of Change: School Leaders of Color Share Narratives of Student, School, and Community Success, pp. xi–xii
Copyright © 2021 by Information Age Publishing

For School Leaders of Color, this leadership imperative is more difficult than it is for our White counterparts. Concomitantly with this leadership necessity are the social and academic disparities of racism, student poverty, lack of resources, just to name a few. Yet many School Leaders of Color have courageously accepted their role to disrupt low performance, and thus they have created environments where students learn and teachers teach. The purpose of this educational preparation supplemental text is to share stories of these exceptional leaders in the field and in the academy.

The experiences shared by the various authors cover four important areas in leadership: Culture and Climate; Student Success; Resilience, Persistence, and Turnaround; and Social Justice. The authors have shared some deeply personal issues and triumphs. As professors of educational leadership, the editors know that these are the stories that resonate more deeply with students and that with these types of stories, the theory to practice bridge is successfully crossed. While many of the chapters include narratives of resilience and triumph in the context of the P–12 education system, the overarching themes and suggestions can be transmuted to any industry. Most importantly, the authors want to convey that leadership is most suited for individuals who desire to make an indelible and intergenerational impact and become a true *Purveyor of Change!*

REFERENCES

Maxwell, J. C. (1993). *Developing the leader within you.* Thomas Nelson.
Nahavandi. (2006). *The art and science of leadership.* Prentice-Hall.

PART I

CULTURE AND CLIMATE

CHAPTER 1

FROM PERIL TO PROMISE

Improving Best Practices for Administrators at Our Nation's Schools

Donna Druery

Bullying behaviors can lead to loss of self-confidence, self-esteem, sleep-lessness, migraines, panic-attacks, and other health and stress-related illnesses (Rayner et al., 2003). There is an overabundance of information regarding bullying that happens to students on school campuses (Cutbush & Williams, 2016; Finkelhor et al., 2015; Fluck, 2017; Sei-Hill, & Telleen, 2017) and how school leaders and counselors can address bullying by students (Austin et al., 2016). However, there is a paucity of evidence and research discussing what happens on school campuses across the nation as it relates to school leaders bullying other school leaders, and even less research when discussing principal leaders bullying other principal leaders on school campuses. I call this administrator to administrator bullying. Adults who are the targets of bullying behavior rarely discuss being bullied. In fact, although workplace bullying is not a new phenomenon, the actual concept of bullying was named a little more than a decade before (Raynor, et al., 2003). However, what happens when the person who is bullying you is your immediate supervisor—and the school principal? Few people want to discuss this issue, but it is a serious issue. This is my personal account of being bullied on campus and what I (finally) had to do about it. Raynor et al. (2003) suggest bullying in the workplace affects working conditions, health and safety, domestic life, and the right of all to equal opportunity and treatment. It is a gradually wearing-down process which makes individuals feel demeaned and inadequate, that they can never get anything right and that they are hopeless within their work environment but also in their domestic life. It can be subtle and devious and often it is difficult for those on the receiving end to confront their perpetrator (p. xi).

Webster's dictionary (2017) defines bullying as abuse and mistreatment of someone vulnerable by someone stronger and more powerful. Across the nation, schools have put antibullying laws in place. Forty-nine states now have antibullying laws (Lamplugh, 2001). Twelve states include a criminal sanction for bullies, ranging from school suspension to jail time (Cyberbullying Research Center, 2013). Texas recently implemented SB 179 on September 1, 2017, also known as David's Law, with regard to changes on how harassment, bullying, and cyberbullying will be addressed in public schools (Canales, 2017). Under SB 179, the school district must notify the parent or guardian of an alleged victim within three days after the incident is reported and notify the parent or guardian of the victim "within a reasonable amount of time after the incident" (Canales, 2017, p. 23). Principals can report the student allegations to the police department and parents can also seek injunctive relief against the perpetrator. These consequences may help stem the tide of student to student bullying. They do very little to stem the tide of administrator to administrator bullying. Further, when the people at the top are friends of the aggressor, reporting or blowing the whistle is tantamount to career suicide as well as ensuring one will not have opportunities to work within the same district. I will discuss types of bullying, then my experience as a victim of administrator to administrator bullying, the changes that occurred after the bullying behaviors were stopped, and will end with what districts can do to end bullying, and finally nuggets of advice.

TYPES OF BULLYING

There are five types of bullying: physical bullying, verbal bullying, cyberbullying, sexual bullying, and emotional or social bullying. Verbal bullying includes teasing, name calling, inappropriate comments, intimidation, taunting, threatening to cause harm. Social bullying is leaving someone out on purpose, telling other people not to be friends with someone, spreading rumors about someone, and embarrassing someone in public (Rayner et al.,

2003). Since I was the recipient of verbal and social bullying, I will discuss the impact this type of bullying had on me personally and professionally.

CAMPUS NOVICE

Before becoming an administrator, I had served four years as a high school English language arts teacher and was considered very successful. After serving as a first-year teacher, I was asked to become the department head for the ninth-grade English Language Arts Department. I requested that a teacher with over 20 years of experience assist me and we became codepartment chairs of the newly named ninth-grade center. I was also asked to assist the school and the district in other endeavors and initiatives and was sent to visit other school districts in Texas and in Miami, Florida. I was instrumental in assisting with teacher duty schedules and was tapped for the district's grow your own principal program. Some teachers ate lunch in my room rather than in the cafeteria. I was confident in my work and my students' scores were second only to my coleader who had been teaching for over 25 years.

ASSISTANT PRINCIPALS, SCHOOL STAFF, AND CLIQUES

In 2004, I was asked to apply for an assistant principal position at a local middle school. Although I was still taking classes and had not completed my master's degree, I applied, and interviewed to get practice for when I got on the job market. To my surprise, I got the job. The school was a nightmare. The principal was absent more days than he was at school and the other two assistant principals were taking bets on whether he would be in on any given day. When the bell rang for in between class dismissal, the students would run screaming through the halls. None of the departments were meeting, and some teachers were not showing up to teach their own classes. I was shocked and appalled that this was going on in this district as we strictly adhered to the rules and regulations on the other campus. The campus was also low-performing for the second year in a row.

The other two assistant principals (APs) and I began to meet to see how we could gain order in the school, first with the teachers, and then with the students. We crafted plans for teachers to be in places they were supposed to be, including on duty and in their classrooms. We divided each discipline and worked with those disciplines. For example, I worked with the English language arts teachers, and did all the testing for the campus. The other APs worked with math, science, and other departments across the campus. That summer, several things occurred. The principal was released from his position and demoted to assistant principal at the school I had just come from. Both APs received positions in other districts, and we had a new principal. I also tried to transfer, but the new principal, I will call her Gail, blocked my transfer, as she would have all new staff for the start of her first school year.

The staff was still angry about all of the changes that and the other APs and I implemented, but more importantly, Texas Education Agency had come to pay a visit and to close the school in one year, if we did not make changes immediately. What happened next occurred over time. Initially, Gail and I worked together, even with hiring a new AP, and ensuring the teachers were on duty and meeting each week in their departments. The campus was predominantly White, and the African American and Latino students were complaining about the partiality in the administration of discipline, specifically the difference in the treatment of Black students and the treatment of White students. I found their complaints to be true. Students of color would show up in my office in tears about the way they were being treated in the classrooms. One example of mistreatment occurred while students were picking up their schedules. When Latino or Black students needed assistance, the history teacher pretended she could not understand what they were saying, so I moved over to assist students in getting their schedules and welcoming them to school.

Little did I know that I had violated their cliques and norms. The verbal and social bullying had begun in earnest. The physical education teacher started a rumor that I was leaving the school. I found this out when other students began asking me if this was true, and when one of the teachers observed the statement being made and let me know that this had indeed occurred. We had a problem with students staying on campus fighting and committing crimes, so students were issued citations for trespassing if they did not leave upon request. However, when a White student received a ticket for trespassing on school grounds I repeatedly told him to leave, I was called into the office because the parents wanted me to say that I had never asked him to leave. I refused to do this and this further angered the White community. I was dismissed from the meeting, but I heard later that the administrator rescinded the consequence for the White student, but not for the African American students. (The White student was later arrested for drug possession.)

A few teachers made a pact to ensure my days on campus were a living Hades and fraught with problems. Student files came up missing from my office. I had to publicly request that teachers not remove files from my office. I finally had to have my secretary tell teachers they had to sign a form to remove a students' file from the office. This stopped the practice of removing files. Then, at least four teachers reported to the superintendent of schools that I was showing favoritism to the African American students and that students were hiding out in my office, refusing to go to class. Fortunately, I had worked with the superintendent and he knew this was not my modus operandi. He punted back to the campus principal to hold a conference with my accusers, who had to face me. When it was proven that their accusations were false, they were made to apologize. I told them I wanted an apology in writing and to carbon copy the Superintendent.

WEEKLY MEETINGS

Each week, the administrative team held weekly meetings and each week, we would discuss the duties and responsibilities for each administrator. The information often included what each of us would discuss at the weekly faculty meeting. When I was given information to discuss with the faculty, invariably Gail would stand up and say the information that I had stated was incorrect (referring to the information I received from the weekly meetings). After several of these occurrences, I stopped reporting out any information. In fact, I refused to speak at the faculty meetings. I spoke only in rare instances at weekly meetings. I typed and took notes only. I became a highly paid secretary, refusing to discuss any information with the faculty, and in essence, I stopped speaking in public spaces, at school meetings and faculty meetings.

We also had another assistant principal who was considered to be one of Gail's favorite people. Any time he requested off, he would receive it. He showed animals professionally and would often have competitions beginning on Fridays. In fact, I would still be on after-school duty many days when he was given permission to leave early get to his competitions. When I would also request permission to leave school, it was rarely granted.

Another employee was booted from another campus by her principal and came to work on our campus as the dean. Trina* and the principal joined together, and the bullying behaviors increased. If I asked a question or made a comment in public spaces, I was ignored. If I asked them in private or made a suggestion, I would receive an answer. If I had an idea, it would be no, but if someone else shared the same idea, that was met with excitement and implementation. Two staff became my allies, and if I made a suggestion, one would begin to discuss the merits of it, the other would suggest that it was a great idea, and that is how we would propose passage of my ideas.

Nonetheless, my self-esteem was at an all-time low. It did no good to report these instances to anyone in central office because the people in the top offices were friends with the principal. There was nowhere to go. I had requested changes to another campus, and it was always refused. I did good work, I was fair to every student, regardless of color. It seemed the principal wanted to keep me on campus to do the work, and to keep me around as campus enforcer, as well as to keep her power over me.

PRAYER USHERS IN CHANGE:
THE TURN-AROUND FACTORS

My pastor often reminds us that "change is inevitable, but prayer ushers in change." Change for the district begin to occur in the form of a new superintendent. When the new superintendent arrived, one of the first things he did was to balance the demographics of the district. Central Office was full of Whites who were all related or friends with one another. The new superintendent, William Russell*, was tough and shrewd. Russell made it clear that he wanted the district's employees to have the same demographics as the school, which were majority Latino and African American. People in Central Office began retiring at high rates and those who did not retire were asked to leave. I remember one day after the new superintendent's arrival, I made a request to leave early for an appointment. I was emphatically told, "No!" in the meeting and in front of others. I then stated, "Whatever [the other AP] is saying to leave, that's what I need to say, because he seems to always keep his appointments." Apparently, Gail realized her ongoing treatment of me could be reported to the new superintendent. Gail came to my office in tears, stating she was sorry, and that if this was reported to central office, "You could have my job!" I responded that I did not want her job, I just wanted her to be fair across the board, which is what I had always wanted her to do.

Eventually, someone reported the situations and bullying behaviors occurring on campus, including the bullying behaviors I had endured. Central office staff visited our campus and asked us questions. I was asked to write a statement. Gail was one of those people who was asked to leave her position. At this point, it was resign or be fired. Gail chose to resign. I worked at the campus another two years after her departure. When I resigned in January to work on my PhD full time, the new principal called an emergency faculty meeting to let the staff know that I was leaving. Some of the teachers cried when I made the announcement. Most of them gave me a standing ovation for the work that I had done with them and on the campus. I had served 11 years, and had been bullied at least 6 of those 11 years. The following year after I left, my friends on that campus called me and told me the majority of the staff left. In fact, every department head resigned and left that campus in May of the same year I had resigned. I have no idea why I had to endure all that I did, but I do know this: There is an end to everything!

DISTRICT AND ADMINISTRATIVE POLICIES

There is a call for district and administrative support when adult bullying occurs. Policies must be in place at the administrative level for all districts across America. These policies should include a process whereby adults can confidentially report bullying behaviors without fear of retributions and demotions. Just as students' reports are investigated, and they are innocent until proven guilty, so too must the aggressor and the victim be given opportunities to provide their information. Adult bullying reports must then be investigated so that both sides can come to an agreement on what should occur after the investigation. As in my case, the perpetrator was made to apologize for her bullying behaviors. She eventually was forced to resign. Thus, consequences should include public and private apologies, written and verbal agreement to cease and desist, and even suspension and job loss if behavior continues.

NUGGETS OF ADVICE

Adult bullying behaviors can occur almost anywhere there is an imbalance of power. Due to behaviors occurring in schools, adults, such as myself, are less likely to report the bullying for a plethora of reasons.

1. The victim must have proof of the occurrences. This includes documentation of each event, including dates and who was present at the time of the bullying. Trust someone on campus to discuss the issues with. Build and cultivate alliances so that you are not alone.
2. The victim should not allow the bullying to go on for too long, as studies have shown this can wreak havoc on an individual's emotional well-being. Try to discuss treatment and boundaries with the aggressor. If necessary, discuss with an impartial individual.
3. If the treatment continues, take copies of all documentation to the district office and request that the bullying behaviors be addressed. State facts as calmly as possible. Request time for reconvening and assurance that district officer will take your concerns seriously. Follow up if the district has not contacted you within a week to seven days.
4. Finally, be persistent as to how you will be treated by the bully. When the bully knows you will face them head on, the behavior may decrease or stop.

According to the Cyberbullying Research Center (2013), we must remember that the kids we serve at school and in our communities sometimes may make poor interpersonal choices, but deep down just want to be believed in, supported, and appreciated for the good they can offer to the world. So, it is also with the adults on campus.

REFERENCES

Austin, S. M., Reynolds, G. P., & Barnes, S. L. (2016). School leadership and counselors working together to address bullying. *Reading Improvement, 53*(4), 188–194.

Canales, R. (2017). Cyberbullying in Texas: What you need to know. *Texas Association of School Administrators Professional Journal Insight, 32*(3), 22–23.

Cutbush, S., & Williams, J. (2016). Teen dating violence, sexual harassment, and bullying among middle school youth: Examining measure imbalance by gender. *Journal of Research on Adolescence, 26*(4), 918–926.

Cyberbullying Research: 2013 Update. (2013, November 20). Retrieved August 12, 2020, from https://cyberbullying.org/cyberbullying-research-2013-update

Bullying. (2017). In *Merriam-Webster.com dictionary*. Retrieved August 12, 2020, from https://www.merriam-webster.com/

Finkelhor, D., Turner, H.A., Shattuck, A., & Hamby, S.L. (2015). Prevalence of childhood exposure to violence, crime, and abuse: Results from the national survey of children's exposure to violence. *JAMA Pediatrics, 169*(8), 746–754.

Fluck, J. (2017). Why do students bully? An analysis of motives behind violence in schools. *Youth & Society, 49*(5). 567–587.

Lamplugh, D. (2001). Foreword. In C. Rayner, H. Hoel, & C. L. Cooper, *Workplace bullying: What we know, who is to blame and what can we do?* (2nd ed.). Taylor and Francis.

Rayner, C., Hoel, H., Cooper, C. L. (2003). *Workplace bullying: What we know, who is to blame, and what we can do?* (2nd. ed.). Taylor and Francis.

Sei-Hill, K., & Telleen, M. W. (2017). Talking about school bullying: News framing of who is responsible for causing and fixing the problem. *Journalism & Mass Communication Quarterly, 94*(3), 725–746.

CHAPTER 2

OUT-OF-SCHOOL SUSPENSIONS IMPACT ON STUDENTS AND LEADERS OF COLOR

Dorothy C. Handfield

"Time on task!"

It was June. We were closely approaching the last days of the 2011–2012 school year. I could tell that the staff members and students were lax and entered summer vacation mode. I reminded everyone to remain focused and to continue working. Nonetheless, I secretly told myself, "The last day of school is not coming quickly enough. I am in desperate need of a break."

At that time, the close of the school year meant retirement parties for staff members, registration of newly enrolled students for the upcoming school year, school-wide award celebrations, moving-up ceremonies, and graduations. Close of the school year also included the mundane task of completing and submitting endless end-of-the-school year reports to our central office. Day after day, I stayed late in order to ensure all of our end-of-the-school year reports were correct and submitted in a timely manner. Some days, I left my office hours after school closed only to continue working at home until the early hours of the morning. Since I left the building after it was dark, my night custodial staff insisted that I go home

Purveyors of Change: School Leaders of Color Share Narratives of Student, School, and Community Success, pp. 11–17
Copyright © 2021 by Information Age Publishing

out of concern for my safety. I always responded, "I cannot go home now. I have so much work to do."

One night, around 6:00 P.M., I went through my usual task of checking off reports that central office confirmed receipt. I had a glimmer of hope as I counted the number of check marks. But a cloud of dismay appeared when I realized that I had an additional report to generate. It was our annual out-of-school suspension report, which delineated the details of each student's out-of-school suspension within the specified school year. This report provided the student's name, gender, grade level, amount of days suspended, and the reason(s) for the suspension.

My plan was to fax the report to central office as quickly as possible, so I could go home for the evening. The report could be electronically generated within seconds. However, at that time of the evening, it felt as if the report took hours to generate and print. When I approached my printer, I quickly counted the number of pages and the number of students who I suspended throughout the school year. I was shocked and embarrassed. I was surprised at the number of students who received multiple suspensions during the school year. Majority of these students were frequent visitors to my office during the course of the school day. I was surprised at the reasons for the suspensions. I suspended students for assault and battery, terroristic threats, fighting, vandalism, weapons possession, stealing, and continued disruptive behavior. I was embarrassed because I was the principal of an elementary school. My students ranged in ages from 3 to 14. I was embarrassed to read the pages of numerous names of Black and Latino students who I subjected to punishment. For a maximum of four school days, I did not permit students to attend school and/or walk onto school property. Pending the actual start date of the out-of-school suspension, the length of some students' suspension extended past four school days if the out-of-school suspension coincided with scheduled school district closures. Bottom line, as a leader of color, I denied students who resembled me the right to attend school and the right to earn an education.

As a sat in my office, I tried to rationalize all the suspensions in spite of my feelings. Prior to viewing our out-of-school suspension report, I prided myself on following our school district's suspension policies and procedures with fidelity. I thought to myself, "It was a rough school year. I am quite sure all these suspensions were justified. The students cannot come into my building and not follow my rules." To prove my point, I generated an out-of-school suspension report for the previous school year. I was mortified. For the 2010–2011 school year, again the report was multiple pages long with multiple names of students of color. We had a pattern. Even though district-level administrators did not ask me to address our dismal suspension rates, I was alarmed at my reactions to our students' behavior. I asked myself, "Am I nurturing our students and teaching them how to resolve conflict before leading to disruptive behavior? Or am I punishing our students with the hopes that there will be an automatic positive change in their behavior?" The most pertinent question that I asked myself was, "If I am aware of the specific students who struggle with demonstrating positive social behavior, what interventions if any were implemented to support these students?" Instead of focusing on how I was going to spend my days relaxing from work, I decided to spend my summer vacation reassessing how to tackle our out-of-school suspension rates for the upcoming school year.

IMPACT OF OUT-OF-SCHOOL
SUSPENSIONS ON STUDENTS OF COLOR

When I issued out-of-school suspensions, I did not realize that my actions perpetuated the disenfranchisement of students of color. Students of color are more likely to experience exclusionary discipline than their White counterparts (Skiba et al., 2014). My punishments also contributed to the beliefs that students of color misbehave at extreme rates, which justified the massive volumes of out-of-school suspensions. There is no evidence that students of color in the same schools or districts engage in more severe behavior that White students, which justified higher rates of suspension or expulsion.

Out-of-school suspensions were emotional for students. I conferenced with every student who I suspended. Consistently in every meeting, students candidly displayed their feelings. Some students cried and begged for my forgiveness. Other students were disappointed in their behavior or disappointed with my reaction with a suspension to their behavior. A few students became irate where school security guards entered my office and deescalated the situation with the student. My students' reaction to out-of-school suspensions substantiates research findings. In lieu of changing students' behavior, punishment causes students to respond with anger and aggression or run away (Skiba, 2014). As a result, students eventually become immune to certain levels of punishment, which results in even longer and more severe punishments (Skiba, 2014).

In addition to the emotional impact that out-of-school suspensions have on students, research has stated the negative impact of out-of-school suspensions on students' academic careers. Out-of-school suspensions are a means to discipline students' disruptive behavior (Noltemeyer et al., 2015). In spite of the schools' efforts to provide a positive learning environment, there is a negative correlation between out-of-school suspensions and student achievement (Noltemeyer et al., 2015). In addition, Skiba (2014) concluded that there is no data supporting how out-of-school suspensions and expulsions reduce disruption or improve school climate. The removal of students from school for disciplinary reasons have negative effects on student outcomes and the learning climate (Skiba, 2014).

Students who drop-out of school, struggle financially in the future. There is a positive correlation between out-of-school suspensions and students' dropout rates (Noltemeyer et al., 2015). In general, in 2012, the unemployment rate for people who were 25 years old and older with only a high school diploma was 8.3% whereas, the unemployment rate for people who were 25 years old and older with a college degree was 4.0% (Baum et al., 2013). For Blacks, the unemployment rate for people 25 years old and older with only a high school diploma was 13.4% and, the unemployment rate of Blacks with a college degree was 11.6% (Baum et al., 2013). In 2011, all people who work full-time year-round and only had a high school diploma earned 14% less than people who work full-time year-round and had some college but no degree (Baum et al., 2013). The median lifetime earnings of people with a high school diploma were 27% lower than the median lifetime earnings of people with an associate degree (Baum et al., 2013).

School discipline policies and/or procedures that address in-school violent behavior may contribute to the school-to-prison pipeline. Christle et al. (2005) reported that there are school characteristics that are associated with risk factors for delinquency. Schools that have percentages of students who engage in board of education violations are schools that have high suspension and dropout rates and low academic rates (Christle et al., 2005). As a result, schools utilize ineffective strategies, such as zero-tolerance policies, to sustain student compliance (Castillo, 2014; Christle et al., 2005). Zero-tolerance policies are predetermined punishments for specific school disciplinary infractions (Castillo, 2014). The implementation of zero-tolerance policies has led to an increase in students' arrests and referrals to the juvenile justice system and a growing number of students entering the juvenile justice system due to a direct referral from the students' schools (Castillo, 2014). There is a trend of African American and Latino low socioeconomic status students being subjected to harsher penalties under zero-tolerance policies than their white counterparts (Castillo, 2014).

IMPACT OF OUT-OF-SCHOOL SUSPENSIONS ON A LEADER OF COLOR

Servant leadership is more than just words. As an educational leader, I committed and described myself as a servant of the students. Servant leadership is leadership that focuses on the needs of the followers, empowers the followers, and supports the followers develop their full human capabilities (Northouse, 2015). If inquired about my occupation, I would proudly state that I have served as a school-based administrator for 13 years in a low-income, urban public school district. While speaking, I put extreme emphasis on the word serve because I want the person who I am speaking with to understand that I became a school-based administrator so I can be of service to the students who were under my leadership. I committed myself to improve students' growth, which includes students' social and emotional needs. Yet, I believed that out-of-school suspensions were the sole means to address students' behavior. I did not have a true conception of what being a leader meant. Most importantly, I did not fully comprehend my roles and responsibilities as a leader of color and a leader of students of color.

My reactions to our students' behavior was a demonstration of coercive and legitimate power. Coercive power is the power that a leader gains due to the leader's capacity to penalize or punish followers and, legitimate power is the power that a leader gains due to the leader's status or formal job authority (Northouse, 2015). I realized that I used coercive and legitimate power in order to rule with fear. I wanted our students to fear a suspension notice in order to behave. At times, I lectured and harassed our students about their misbehavior with no remorse. I constantly told students that my authority permitted me to discipline them. In hindsight, I am cognizant that my actions as a leader were not my demeanor as a person. I want to be an educational leader who has the capability to make insightful and equitable decisions on behalf of our students, not an educational leader who struck fear in our students in order to gain control of the school building.

I envisioned myself as a transformational leader. Transformational leadership is the ability as a leader to engage with followers and create a connection that raises the level of motivation and morality in both the leader and the follower (Northouse, 2015). Transformational leadership incorporates intellectual stimulation, where the leader encourages the followers to be creative and innovative and to challenge their own beliefs and values as well as the beliefs and values of the leader and organization (Northouse, 2015). Transformational leadership also infuses individualized consideration that allows the leader to create a supportive climate in which the leaders listen carefully to the individual needs of the followers (Northouse, 2015). The leader is a coach and adviser to the followers while the followers reach their full potential within the organization (Northouse, 2015). In order to truly embrace the theory of transformational leadership, I had to empower the staff members. Disruptive student behavior was not just my problem; it was a school-wide problem. A school-wide problem that required a collaboration of all school-wide staff members. Over the years,

I never had an issue with the staff members questioning and/or challenging my beliefs. We developed a relationship where the staff members and I were able to debate with each other regarding issues and/or concerns in a respectful manner. I did not take the staff members' comments as a personal attack. Despite the staff members being able to challenge my beliefs and/or values, I did not permit the staff members to be creative or innovative and implement ideas that could solve problems within the building. I was stuck on doing things my way regardless if the procedure worked or not. Encouraging staff members to be creative, it was a means to improve their performance. Dictating the actions of the staff, stagnated staff members' potential.

Finally, I want to be a transformational leader who has behavioral integrity. I worked diligently to practice what I preached. If I expected our students to adhere to the policies and procedures of our school, I understood that the expectations that I set for the students I had to adhere to myself. Thus, I had to self-reflect on my behavior.

CONCLUSION

At the completion of the 2012–2013 school year, there was a 50% reduction in our out-of-school suspension rate. Unfortunately, I still suspended students. Nevertheless, the suspensions were not a result of my abuse of power. The suspensions were consequences to students' actions and included a myriad of supportive services so the students could learn how to prevent future infractions. As a staff, we transitioned from a reactive approach to a proactive approach in terms of our disciplinary procedures. We identified and targeted students who needed social and emotional support. These students had regularly scheduled counseling sessions with either the social worker, guidance counselor, and/or crisis teacher. We also collaborated with outside resources in order to provide additional support services. For example, students who experienced the loss of a loved one and/or family member received grief counseling from an outside clinical social worker. Finally, we utilized an "all hands on deck" approach. All staff members were expected to become involved and engaged with our students regardless of the staff members' title. This approach allowed our male staff members to play an integral role in our students' lives, especially our male students. No longer did I demand the students to follow the rules or face out-of-school suspension. I changed my mindset and collaborated with staff members. We, along with the students, constructed proactive programs that focused on the social and/or emotional needs of students.

Due to an unexpected experience during the close of the school year, I have a truer concept of the type of leader that I want to be. I used my inabilities to address students' behavior as an opportunity to reinvent myself as a leader who wholeheartedly wants to bring about change for all students, especially students of color.

REFERENCES

Baum, S., Ma, J., & Payea, K. (2013). Education pay 2013: The benefits of higher education for individuals and society. *The College Board*.

Castillo, J. (2014). Tolerance in schools for Latino students: dismantling the school-to-prison pipeline. *Harvard Journal of Hispanic Policy, 26*, 43.

Christle, C. A., Jolivette, K., & Nelson, C. M. (2005). Breaking the school to prison pipeline: Identifying school risk and protective factors for youth delinquency. *Exceptionality, 13*(2), 69–88.

Noltemeyer, A. L., Ward, R. M., & Mcloughlin, C. (2015). Relationship between school suspension and student outcomes: A meta-analysis. *School Psychology Review, 44*(2), 224.

Northouse, P. G. (2015). *Leadership: Theory and practice*. SAGE.

Skiba, R. J. (2014). The failure of zero tolerance. *Reclaiming children and youth, 22*(4), 27.

Skiba, R. J., Arrondondo, M. I., & Rauch, M. K. (2014). *New and developing research on disparities in discipline*. Discipline Disparities: A Research to Practice Collaborative. The Atlantic Philanthropies.

CHAPTER 3

YOU'RE HIRED!

An Administrator's Tale of Attracting, Training, and Retaining Highly Qualified Teachers

Lawrence Scott

Being a teacher in today's public school system can be severely overwhelming! Correspondingly, being an administrator, especially an administrator of color, can often feel insurmountable. Many administrators of color are placed in high-need (high-poverty, vulnerable) turnaround schools, solely as disciplinarians, without adequate resources, latitude to fire subpar faculty and staff, and little time to create successful results due to high turnover rates of teachers and principals (Forte, 2014; Murakami et al., 2018). According to Duke (2006), the major components present in a turnaround school are as follows: *assistance, collaboration, data-driven decision making, leadership, organization structure, staff development, curriculum alignment, high expectations, parental involvement, and scheduling.* Regrettably, many administrators in high poverty schools spend an inordinate amount of time on discipline issues. Their focus on closing achievement gaps, or differentiated instructional modalities, is eclipsed by classroom management

Purveyors of Change: School Leaders of Color Share Narratives of Student, School, and Community Success, pp. 19–28
Copyright © 2021 by Information Age Publishing
All rights of reproduction in any form reserved.

issues. Many would blame the students for the challenging behaviors. I purport that great administrators will hire and adequately train teachers that will implement instructional strategies from a well-planned lesson that will facilitate complete student engagement and participation. In those classes, students are master contributors to the learning experience. Outside of this model, administrators will be called to handle "discipline problems," usurping the power of the teacher, and robbing the student of optimal content area exposure.

I'M NOT YOUR DISCIPLINARIAN!
I'M AN INSTRUCTIONAL LEADER TOO

This chapter means a great deal to me because I became an administrator to make systemic changes. I learned in my first week that my role was relegated to a disciplinarian. Many high poverty school districts are particularly amenable to hiring administrators of color as purveyors of discipline and not purveyors of academic or instructional change. As if they become an overseer on the plantation to quell the insurrection of the slaves by rewarding docility, while extirpating empowerment. In this model, as Freire (1972) has chronicled, the oppressed becomes the oppressor once they are given autonomy in a position. These administrators are usually seen as disciplinarians meant to "clean up" discipline issues instead of an instructional leader. These leaders will spend the majority of their day talking to students and parents about discipline issues, or their faculty and staff on classroom management techniques, as opposed to using data to create a plan for resource allocation and implementation of best instructional practices for optimal student learning and academic achievement. Ultimately, these administrators may feel a sense of burn-out as they sedulously work toward academic, school culture and climate, and community-based goals with little to no resolve.

I vividly remember the phone conversations I had with some of my educational mentors who have led schools (Dr. Mateen Diop, Dr. Sean Kearney, Dr. Milton Fields, Dr. Willie Black, and Dr. Ron Kelley), and who all encouraged me to find time and energy to be an instructional leader and not just a disciplinarian or a building manager. They helped me see that I could be an active participant in the elimination of disproportionality in discipline practices for our Black and Latinx students, as well as shape instruction in the classroom. Keeping that perspective was difficult as I saw a girl who hit me across my head in the cafeteria be released from liability because it was connected to her 504 disability. Also, I found out that she had previously assaulted several teachers prior to my arrival at that campus.

Even though I was assaulted and issued death threats more times as an administrator than I had in the previous 15 years in education, I knew the change had to start at the top. I vocalized my sentiment to my immediate supervisors and they simply asserted that in high need schools, they need administrators that can handle a great deal of discipline issues. This situation certainly exasperated my teachers as I was getting over 30 referrals a day and unable to handle every situation satisfactorily. Duke and Landahl (2011) suggested that real change requires at least 3 years, which gives the principal enough time to implement comprehensive, organizational change. Sadly, many of these administrators are promoted if they achieve their academic goals, or reassigned, demoted, or resign if the district and campus objectives are not met. For the purpose of this chapter, we will examine some methods of hiring, training, and retaining high quality educators from research-based and anecdotal personalized experiences.

LEADERS HIRE LEADERS

Great school leadership can be the difference between a school that experiences marginal success and a school that sustains high student achievement, high community involvement, and teacher retention and satisfaction. What makes a great school leader? In my 17 years in public education as an educator, curriculum specialist, and guidance counselor, particularly in a high poverty school district, I have seen many leaders with positional power, but lacked influence. Referencing the French and Raven's Bases of Power Model as analyzed by Nahavandi (2006), I have seen those with influence but lacked the title, but knew how to build consensus, create and operationalize a concerted plan, and monitor and adjust when necessary. World renowned leadership trainer John Maxwell (1998) uses the word *power* interchangeably with *influence*. Using Maxwell's framework of influence, with the backdrop of French and Raven's sources of power, the school leadership supersedes titles and positions and presupposes that those with referent (reverence) and expert (knowledge) powers may possess more influence than those with an actual title or position (legitimate, coercive, reward powers). This keen understanding and discernment earlier in my career gave me the desire to expand my abilities to create systemic change. I realized that my classroom I conveniently labeled "Zone of Success," was a small microcosm of change that can be done beyond my classroom walls. I decided to get my principalship certification and become a secondary administrator.

Doing a cursory inventory of what principals did, and recounting the various principals I experienced as a teacher and even a student, I knew being an administrator would require a charismatic speaker, a change agent, a manager of systems and people, a leader that could consolidate resources, and transform schools. While all these attributes are needed, my personal experience of becoming an administrator began with a paradigmatic shift. My first week on campus we had more than eight physical fights. There were times when I would call the parents to pick up the students after being suspended due to the mutual combat and the parents would try to fight each other. Many nights our referees from the basketball games had to be escorted by police. Even amid the chaos, most of our students were happy to come to school because they were guaranteed a hot meal and a place to belong. Unfortunately, there were some students who, due to their precipitating circumstances, could never make our campus an extension of their home. This is why I sought after mission-minded, highly qualified teachers.

HIGH QUALITY EDUCATORS DEFINED

In my experience, many urban schools are insufficiently equipped to adjust to the perennial malaise endemic of societal and systemic changes. Many students entered our schools reading below grade level (low Lexile levels), victimized by intergenerational poverty, and unable to adequately adapt to the social-cultural context and linguistic acquisition necessary for academic success. Teachers needed to completely differentiate instruction to meet the varied needs of all students in a classroom. In one classroom, a teacher could have students who were in the special education, English as a second language (ESL), 504 Plan for Those with Dyslexia, gifted and talented, advanced placement, and "general education" programs. While this may seem like a daunting task, the most highly qualified teachers I have recommended for employment or witnessed throughout my educational career were not only up to the challenge, but knew instinctively how to consolidate resources to make success inevitable in their classrooms for their students.

These teachers were successful because they knew pedagogical content and how to employ multiple modalities to serve every student's learning needs (Gardner, 1993; Manner, 2001; Schrand, 2008). Similar to the special education program, each student had an Individual Education Plan (IEP). These teachers would invest time in each student, attend their games, recitals, family gatherings, and churches. These teachers would embed themselves in the community so that when a student or parent was murdered in the community, many times these teachers were called upon by the families to speak on behalf of the school. These teachers were the *Purveyors of Change*.

DIFFICULTIES IN THE HIRING PROCESS

Since I was an administrator in a school district in which 91% of the students were economically disadvantaged (based on the number of free or reduced lunch), it was my job as an administrator to locate those teachers that were community and mission-minded. Unfortunately, if you were desiring to hire teachers of color, especially Black male teachers for a school with a high concentration of Black students, there were some difficulties. With only 2% of all teachers in America Black males, there were some viable ways to recruit teachers within the P–20 pipeline (Bristol & Goings, 2019; Goings & Bianco, 2016). It absolutely starts with encouraging males in the undergraduate programs to pursue advanced degrees to create a teacher-leader pipeline for Black males (Scott & Sharp, 2019). Nonetheless, due to the nature of the schools we were serving, we were thankful for any teachers that would apply and interview.

On the surface, this seemed like an easy task. You would interview teachers and evaluate them by their ability to answer the questions from the committee. Unfortunately, I was fooled by several teachers as they were able to answer questions adequately by giving rehearsed, memorized answers for the generalized questions provided. Toward the end of my stint as an administrator, and even now as full-time faculty member at the university level, who has been on several search committees, I now employ a different set of philosophical and application-based questions that would allow me to ascertain how applicants would react in certain situations. I would ask them what motivated them to go into the educational profession. I would inquire about the last two to three books, conference workshops or seminars they thoroughly enjoyed. I would even ask them to do a mock lesson or simulation. One time, when hiring a social worker and counselor on our team, we invited one of our very challenging student leaders to converse with the applicant after the interview. We wanted to see how he would interact with a student who did not look or even act like the prototypical scholar. Little did the applicant know, even though the student was involved in gangs, he was wildly emotionally intelligent, and could discern whether this counselor would do well with our student population. The applicant did well and was recommended for the position the next day.

RETAINING HIGHLY QUALIFIED EDUCATORS

As an administrator, I would first meet all my staff individually to understand their needs and motivations. By the end of the 1st week, I knew why they decided to become educators, their family constellation (if they volunteered the information), what motivated them, what type of leader they wanted to be, and their personal and professional goals. As an administrator, I employed Hershey and Blanchard's Situational Leadership (Navahandi, 2006). For my highly qualified teachers who had the will and skill to educate our students, I would endeavor to give them everything they needed to be successful and move out of their way (delegating). For those who had the will but lacked the skill, I would coach them (coaching). For teachers who had the skill, but lacked the will, I knew I needed to support their endeavors more and build leadership capacity and density (supporting). For those who lacked the will and skill, I knew their days were numbered and encouraged them to *grow or go* (directing).

Even teachers that struggled for the first few years, I took a coaching rather than punitive approach to help them transition to become a better educator. We assigned them teacher mentors to help them transition. Most teachers in this situation would humbly seek to learn methods of improving their instruction. There were a few that I saw either lacked the desire to grow in their profession, which translated to me that they were unwilling to do whatever it took to provide optimal instruction and educational opportunities to our students. I had one teacher who literally told me and the administrative staff that she was not going to implement the suggested strategies because she felt that our administrative staff would change the next year. For these kinds of teachers, I understood their game, and knew it was only a matter of time before they were terminated or decided to resign. As Abraham Lincoln said, "You can fool all the people some of the time, and some of the people all the time, but you cannot fool all the people all the time."

Many times, in high-needs schools, teachers were placed there because they were unable to perform at other schools, and principals or districts would pass the problem to another school. The hope was either to inspire them to perform better in another environment under another leader, or help the district make a cogent decision for termination based on the documentation from different leaders. My goal was to give teachers the benefit of the doubt. It would usually take a novice teacher 3 years to become acclimated to the classroom. Most of the schools in which I was an administrator or guidance counselor, had a great deal of new teachers, usually straight out of college, or from Teach for America (TFA). If they were TFA, and were transformative leaders on campus, I knew I had two years to convince them to continue in our field if this was their purpose. In my previous district, we were able to retain a little over 53% of the TFA teachers after the 2-year threshold. I learned from the teaching of Pastor Keith Graham that "Teachers do not leave schools or students, or even their purpose, teachers leave *Relationships and Leadership*." Research suggest that teacher retention is increased when teachers are working collaboratively with their colleagues for a common purpose, receive appropriate professional development, and are treated with unparalleled respect (Callahan, 2016; Chenoweth & Theokas, 2013).

To retain the best teachers, removing barriers that impeded their ability to teach was paramount. This coincided with the (Path Goal Theory) which suggest that leaders must locate and remove possible barriers that will preclude teacher performance. Whether it was classroom management challenges, lack of content enrichment, or just overall feelings of overwhelm, principal and school leaders need to be able to identify and eliminate imminent threats of instructional success. To many times, the best teachers who had the most campus and community influence were asked to do more than their counterparts. Whether it was the Campus Leadership Team, Site Based Decision Making Team, Response to Intervention group, Parent Teacher Association, or after school interventions, these teachers were given more activities that minimized their lesson and curriculum planning time, as well as simple rest and recharge. This is where your educational leadership style is paramount. Knowing how to help your teachers grow, without overusing or burning out the most participatory or effective teachers, is a hybrid of art and science, which goes back to the aforementioned Hershey and Blanchard's Situational Leadership Theory (Navahandi, 2006).

TEACHER TRAINING

In addition to making sure my teachers had more than adequate supplies, I needed to make sure they were effectively trained so their students can have more than adequate instructional results. I vividly recall an exchange between a teacher and a parent in which the teacher (who was White) felt the parent (who was Black) was being hostile and irate. After the parent conference, I let her know that some of our parents may be more expressive and does not necessarily intimate aggression. As educators, we have to be sensitive to these cultural cues. I needed to make sure all faculty and staff had the best training in both culturally responsive teaching and crisis responsive training (CRTs). I needed to make sure, that no matter the social or economic malady of their students, they were able to reach and educate ALL students. Nonetheless, when teachers feel supported by their administration, especially with regards to their educational competencies, teachers are able to lead their students to optimal levels of learning. Teachers that are supported share in the contribution and autonomy of the campus goals, vision, and trajectory. Here in Texas, most public schools begin with a Comprehensive Needs Assessment (CNA) that will propel their Campus Improvement Plan (CIP) which will ultimately decide how your funds will be allocated. Whether its professional development, supplies, tutoring initiatives, classroom technological integration, this is the incipient stage that prioritizes what content areas will be funded and to what degree.

TENETS FOR LEADERS

Is there a panacea or elixir for administrators that guarantees attracting the most highly qualified, mission-minded teachers? Not likely, but here are some more supportive, yet anecdotal things that helped me as an administrator to build a campus culture and climate of success inside my schools and their surrounding communities.

1. **Inspire to Be**—Be the leader that you would love to work with and for.
2. **Hire for Passion, Train for Content Enrichment**—Some of the most knowledgeable teachers I've met were not passionate about students, particularly students from the communities in which I was called to serve. Later, I learned to hire for passion, and train for content perfection. If you have an applicant with a hybrid of both, hire them immediately.
3. **Empower and Delegate**—The role of an administrator is to empower their teachers to become leaders inside and outside the classroom. If you are doing ALL the work, you have not built leadership capacity and density in your staff that will create a culture and climate of growth.
4. **Take Care of Teachers First**—Too many times I have seen administrators try to be there for all students. While this is important, your job as a leader is to support your teachers so they can support your students.
5. **Build Relationships**—Just like every teacher should know their students by name and educational need, administrators need to know their teachers by name and need. Also, building community relationships such as the local businesses is paramount as they can help you with incentives or mentors for your students for your dedicated celebratory items.
6. **Influence at ALL Levels**—John Maxwell (2006), talks about being a 360-degree leader which entails influencing those below you, your contemporaries that are laterally positioned, and your superiors.
7. **Celebrate all Success**—When teachers are appreciated, students will feel appreciated (supports learning). Even celebrating the small successes (scores on benchmarks, attendance goals met, discipline referral reduction) will help the team refocus on the ultimate goals set by the campus leadership team.

8. **Get Advice**—Some of the best administrators I have experienced have no qualms calling people in their social network to assist them. We all do not know everything, and every school year, classroom, teacher, student, presents new challenges that cannot be met with yesterday's solutions.

9. **Solve Problems**—You were hired and will continue to rise based on your ability to solve a problem. Whether its low standardized scores, dropout rates, low graduation or completion rates, discipline issues—every problem has a solution. Your job is to identify the problem, build the team necessary to address the problem, and make it happen.

10. **Make No Decision in a Vacuum**—always build consensus and collaboration when possible. Of course, time does not permit the democratization of all decisions, but this is when your delegated authority is critical.

11. **Plan and Prioritize**—Since you know there will be a superfluity of challenges (buses arriving late, cafeteria running out of food, pipe burst on the second floor, power outages, parent/student fighting at a football game) you have to know what requires your attention first.

12. **Stay Decisive**—There will be times you will be tired of making decisions. Nevertheless, so many people rely on your ability to make a cogent, data supported decision.

13. **Reflect and Reevaluate on Progress**—Successful school leaders always find ways to measure success by the achievement of the concerted vision and goals of the campus. Great leaders follow-up, keep themselves and everyone else accountable, and find ways to use data to support improvement and elimination of achievement gaps.

REFERENCES

Bristol, T. J., & Goings, R. B. (2019). Exploring the boundary-heightening experiences of Black male teachers: Lessons for teacher education programs. *Journal of Teacher Education, 70*(1), 51–64.

Callahan, J. J. (2016). Encouraging retention of new teachers through mentoring strategies. *Delta Kappa Gamma Bulletin, 83*(1), 6–11.

Chenoweth, K. K., & Theokas, C. C. (2013). How high-poverty schools are getting it done. *Educational Leadership, 70*(7), 56–59.

Duke, D. L. (2006). What we know and don't know about improving low-performing schools. *Phi Delta Kappan, 87*(10), 729–734.

Duke, D. L., & Landahl, M. (2011). Raising test scores was the easy part: A case study of the third year of school turnaround. *International Studies in Educational Administration, 39*(3), 91–114.

Forte, L. (2014). Slowing the revolving door. *Catalyst in Depth, 25*(3), 2.

Freire, P. (1972). *Pedagogy of the oppressed*. Penguin.

Gardner, H. (1993) *Multiple intelligences: The theory in practice*. Basic Books.

Goings, R. B., & Bianco, M. (2016). It's hard to be who you don't see: An exploration of Black male high school students' perspectives on becoming teachers *Urban Review, 48*(4), 628–646.

Manner, B. (2001). Learning styles and multiple Intelligences in students: Getting the most out of your students' learning. *Journal of College Science Teaching, 30*(6), 390–393.

Murakami, E., Kearney, W. S., Scott, L., & Alfaro, P. (2018). An examination of one high-poverty/high minority school in need of improvement. *International Studies in Educational Administration, 46*(1), 3–22.

Maxwell, J. (1998) *The 21 irrefutable laws of leadership*. Thomas Nelson.

Maxwell, J. (2006) *The 360-degree leader*. Thomas Nelson.

Nahavandi. (2006). *The art and science of leadership*. Prentice-Hall

Schrand, T. (2008). Tapping into active learning and multiple intelligences with interactive multimedia: A low-threshold classroom approach. *College Teaching, 56*(2), 78–84.

Scott, L., & Sharp, L. A. (2019). Educational attainment of advanced degrees among Black males: An exploration of critical factors that promote and preclude success. *Journal of Negro Education, 88*(1), 44–61.

CHAPTER 4

SELLING EDUCATION

Charisma S. Popillion

Those who serve in education are called to the task of laying the foundation for our adults of tomorrow. For some of us in this field, it has been no easy task creating a sense of urgency and motivational tactics, but it is worth every effort. We find ourselves in the position of having to sell the meaning and benefits of education to our clients who are our students and parents.

I have served in the field of education for over 15 years, with the privilege of working as a classroom teacher, curriculum coordinator, assistant principal, district special programs coordinator, and currently a campus principal. Throughout my entire career, I have worked on campuses which are considered Title I campuses. These campuses have a vast population of the student body which is affected by poverty-stricken conditions. Funds are provided to the campus to help ensure that all children meet state standards and are academically successful.

The campus I currently lead services kindergarten through fifth grade students. There are 33 teachers serving students on this campus. The demographic make-up of the school is currently 70% African American, 25% Hispanic, and 5% Asian, White, and American Indian. Last year, the school was in the third year of improvement required status due to not meeting indices 1 and 3 in our state accountability rating system, which relate to our overall student performance and closing achievement gaps.

Purveyors of Change: School Leaders of Color Share Narratives of Student, School, and Community Success, pp. 29–34
Copyright © 2021 by Information Age Publishing

When a school does not meet state accountability for 4 to 5 consecutive years, the campus could ultimately be repurposed and taken over by the state.

A common theme I have found while working in this field is the lack of motivation and sense of urgency when it comes to education. The lack does not stop and start with the students. I have witnessed it travel from the community to the home, and then from school personnel to the student. Everyone knows the popular statement, "It takes a village to raise a child." Well, this still holds true. In order for students to complete school as well-rounded productive citizens, the community must play an integral role in developing school-aged children. It requires the community to speak on the power and benefits of education. The mantra, "Education is Power" should be spoken in churches, paraphernalia posted in community stores, barber shops, beauty, and nail salons, as well as in restaurants. The message must be delivered that not one person can be successful without an adequate education.

Unfortunately, since this message is not what is always relayed, and parents have had their own educational experiences, some not so great, children suffer. Some parents feel intellectually inadequate and therefore do not feel comfortable coming to the schools for parent—teacher conferences, nor do they show up for educational family nights. When parents feel disconnected and do not see the "power of education" message relayed continuously, there is a weak educational connection which, if stronger, could foster dynamic academic growth with students.

When educational messages are spread during Sunday church services, and when honor roll grades are posted at church and in the local businesses, then and only then will the message begin to resonate in the home and community that education is foundational to success. In the school and community, parents must be supported and encouraged with a sense of urgency to take part and be involved in their child's educational experiences. They will then feel a sense of purpose and power in their child's academic success.

Education is a civil right. In the schools in which I have served, and for many across the state and nation, there is an achievement gap. Research has proven that our Caucasian counterparts are consistently outperforming our African American students (Ferrer & Garlington, 2012). This can be attributed to a number of factors including economic status, parents' level of education, and the presence of literature in the homes. My experience has shown that in many cases, motivation, and the sense of urgency for education are prevalent in the homes of our Caucasian students.

When I completed my student teaching in a predominantly Caucasian elementary school, I worked with first graders. All the students were reading at or above their current grade level and had comprehension skills well above their skill expectancy. Subsequently, I started my teaching career at a predominantly African American middle school. I was assigned to work with sixth and eighth graders teaching reading and English. After the first lesson with my students, I knew there was a discrepancy. My first graders, whom I had worked with the year prior, were reading at a higher level than my sixth and eighth grade students. I know brain capacity is not determined by zip code, so I knew those students across town were no smarter than the students I had in my classroom, but the key component was motivation and a sense of urgency that unfortunately did not come from the home. Reading with children every night, ensuring they completed their homework, and reviewing skills and concepts would be characterized as a sense of urgency.

This is when I realized that relationships would be vital in my role as an educator. I then learned that my role was not only a teacher, it would be a role model, a mother figure, a nurse, a counselor, but most importantly, a saleswoman. At this point, I had a revelation. Just as one may travel door to door to sell a Kirby vacuum cleaner to someone who does not know the importance of this vacuum cleaner, what it is capable of doing, the benefits of it, how it can make life easier, and how it can serve as an investment, I would have to sell education to my students and parents. I would have to help foster a sense of urgency and help to motivate the students and parents in the community in which I served and continue to serve every day.

I began to work very hard at building relationships with students as well as parents. The saying holds true that "one does not care how much you know until they know how much you care" (Maxwell, 1998). I showed an interest in the students' lives. I took the opportunity while teaching reading and writing to make the literature and lessons relevant, come alive and have meaning to the students. I invited parents to celebrate their children's success. I held tutorials after school, and even became a sponsor for after-school activities so that I could be present and have those one-on-one conversations with parents and students.

In my current position as a principal, I continue to do the same. When we hold Saturday school, it is not a time for parents to drop off students and go about their morning. They are expected to come as well. No, this is not the time when we simply give flyers and talk about the standards and expectations of state mandated assessments. This is a time where we conduct meaningful activities for our parents. We allow parents to create vision boards. With the population in which I serve, many parents are given the stigma that they do not care. This is far from the truth. Many of our parents lack motivation because they were not motivated and did not have any meaningful source of motivation themselves. No one fostered this in them, and it has become a vicious cycle. Many do not feel comfortable speaking their truths and feelings, so we provide opportunities to do it in various ways. Through the vision board activity, parents are given several magazines and other literature in which they can find images and words which depict their feelings, wishes, and dreams for their children and family. It has been an eye-opening experience for all involved. And simply having their parents there at the school, learning and working while they are learning and working has a monumental impact on the motivation and encouragement of our students. We have to be intentional in the ways in which we reach out to our parents and students.

Due to the reading deficits in our schools and community, literacy movements are integral in building foundational reading skills. We must shift the paradigm that reading is not fun. We must stress that reading is foundational, can be fun, and can be a basis of pulling families together. Literacy nights are amazing ways to involve whole families in the literary movement. "Bring Dad to Story Night" was a way my current campus brought together our community partners, business partners, dads, uncles, cousins, and brothers to take part in pushing the literacy movement. We also encourage our students to read during any down-time at school, such as waiting in line at the restroom, after they have finished their lunch in the cafeteria, and waiting during after-school dismissal. We offer tangible, as well as intangible incentives for reading accomplishments, such as collecting an abundance of points for reading certain books and completing an assessment over the book.

Our campus' student population is one-fourth Hispanic, so therefore we have inclusive approaches to all events. During the events that we hold, we are sure to provide translators, as well as multicultural materials and topics. Although our Hispanic students traditionally outperform our African American students, they continually suffer reading deficits and sometimes lack motivation as well.

In the spring semester of every year, our state-mandated exam, the State of Texas Assessment of Academic Readiness (STAAR), quickly approaches. During the assessment season, we begin to see students suffer with physical and mental health issues as a result of the anticipation of these assessments. To combat this issue, we have decided that we would hold morning motivational meetings. Every Monday, Tuesday, and Wednesday morning, our leadership team holds what we call "STAAR Family Meetings." We play motivational songs and give words of encouragement from the principal and other leadership team members. We provide reminders of the importance of attendance and positive behavior choices, a review of specific academic strategies, and positive reinforcements from our campus counselor. At times, teachers and students create chants and other simple skits to share with the other students. These meetings last no longer than 20 minutes. We feel that in the case that no one has provided the motivation, encouragement, and excitement for education, we would dedicate ourselves to ensuring that it happens for each one of our students. No one could ever know what type of living conditions and experiences our students face each day. The school is to be a place of refuge for our students where they feel safe, important, and encouraged. This is our call. This is our duty.

As a teacher in the classroom, I came to the realization that I had the capability to be labeled a superhero. I had the power in my hands to mold a child's future. It was up to me while that child was in my reach to do everything I could to ensure I unlocked all sense of urgency, actively motivated, and interceded on his or her behalf.

Teachers must take the time to design culturally-responsive lessons which increase mastery learning, embedded with research-based instructional strategies. Lessons must allow students to make connections through meaningful and relevant experiences. Students will eventually feel a desire to learn, which will ultimately create motivated students who feel a sense of urgency in regard to their education and future. This holds true at all levels of education.

Leadership teams must monitor the productivity of time and effective usage of the resources provided for instruction. Professional development in the areas of adequate lesson planning and differentiation must occur in order for teachers to reach the level of rigor needed for student success. The usage of classroom management techniques and instructional strategies that promote student engagement and high achievement are especially important in ensuring student success. Teachers must provide opportunities for students to work in small groups and make connections with the real-world using hands-on learning experiences.

Furthermore, professional development in working with children of poverty must be addressed, inclusively of all staff members. Leaders must not turn a blind eye to the disconnection which happens all too often when educators are not connected and have not formed relationships with their students, and the students in turn suffer. The students in which we serve learn in many different ways. They not only possess multiple intelligences, they have different learning styles which, if not acknowledged by educators, will cause students to fail irrevocably. When a student is not "getting it," we must teach the way they learn. So many times, I have heard teachers state, "I taught that concept," "I taught that skill." My question for them is, "Did they learn it?" We must move beyond teaching curriculum to teaching "students."

In order for this problem to be addressed, all educators must set high expectations for themselves and others. The state of Texas has added student progress to the evaluation of teachers. When students show growth, it will inevitably reveal the growth of teachers. Teachers are expected to create student learning objectives where they track student progress with specificity in order to meet student needs.

Leadership teams must expect the best from teachers and be prepared to face resistance when faced with push back and non-compliance. Serving as a campus principal, I believe I have had more experiences and learned more than some principals do in their first five years; however, I will never cease learning how to reach the unreachable, touch the untouchable, and do the unthinkable to be sure that all students leave our campus well on their way to being productive citizens.

Songs we have played for our students tell them they are the world's greatest, there is no stopping them, and we love them so much. My first year at my current campus, I started what we call the "Annual Bulldog Walk." At the end of the second semester of school, our fifth grade students march to a memorial built by the alumni association of the high school in which we are named after about three blocks away from the school. This memorial was built to honor the school and community. Each student takes this walk to symbolize the journey of hardships and trials they may have endured to get where they are at that very moment. Staff members chaperone and serve as coaches to support and ensure their safety, but also to encourage them to take every step carefully and closely while reminding them not to step off their path to their ending elementary destination.

As vehicles and pedestrians pass throughout the neighborhood, their neighborhood I might add, we remind them not to ever get distracted. Despite someone approaching them, and offering something very appealing, we stress to stay the course. The race will be won by the person who never lost his or her focus and faith. This event is meaningful to the adults as well. When it is all said and done, we remind our staff, community, and business partners "to the world, you may be one person, but to one person, you may be the world." Be the encouragement. Be the motivation. Be the light. Be the sense of urgency. Education has developed into a business and we have a quota to meet, with our product being student success.

REFERENCES

Ferrer, L., & Garlington, S. (2012). *Voices*. DuPage County Regional Office of Education.

Maxwell, J. (1998). *The 21 irrefutable laws of leadership*. Thomas Nelson.

PART II

STUDENT SUCCESS

CHAPTER 5

"CAUSE YOU TALK LIKE ME"

Color'd Girl Leading

Patricia Virella

Being alive and being a woman is all I got but being colored is a
metaphysical dilemma I haven't conquered yet.

—Shange (1974)

'Cause you talk like me.

—Cielo, 9-year-old

In 2015, I became the third principal in three years, inheriting an all-girls
charter school with consistently low enrollment, dismal state test scores, and
a high suspension rate. While these issues were pressing, I quickly realized
that there was a more urgent issue that needed to be addressed—the social
and emotional needs of our girls. This need was revealed in a conversation
with a fourth grader named Cielo. As we walked down the hallway, early
in September, we talked about being back at school. She remarked that
she liked me and was happy I was her principal. I asked, "Why?" and she
replied, " 'Cause you talk like me." Her answer startled me. Cielo, a young
Puerto Rican girl began to tell me stories about her teachers, mostly white

*Purveyors of Change: School Leaders of Color Share Narratives of Student, School, and
Community Success*, pp. 37–40
Copyright © 2021 by Information Age Publishing

women, who did not understand the Lower East Side neighborhood she came from. Teachers would call school safety officers when someone was not listening or have the dean waiting outside her classroom to remove a fellow student. For her, it was not a matter of them not caring, but the lack of understanding that she felt was present.

Hearing her honest words made me realize, that as the principal of this school, I had to examine how the teachers and students engaged with each other. To accomplish this task, I engaged in a year long process which would challenge my own notion of how my identity would influence my leadership activities. Given the success of this process in this chapter I describe my experiences being an Afro-Latina leader and how I shifted the policing culture of this school to an equitable and culturally relevant environment. First, I describe how I shifted the culture, then I explain the barriers of enacting my plan. Finally, I conclude with the benefits of the shift and how I was impacted as a leader.

PLANS TO CHANGE

Immediately after my conversation with Cielo, I took action. I began by writing an e-mail to my midlevel leaders explaining the concern I had regarding how we treated our students. I relayed Cielo's story and other observations I made over the course of the first few weeks of the new school year. I explained that as a leadership team we would need to build the capacity of social-emotional understanding across the school. Additionally, I committed to the goal of suspensions being dramatically reduced. We would only suspend students in the case of grave danger such as bringing a weapon to school. My goal was to convey to my staff and leaders that as an elementary school with 99% female students of color, we would not continue the oppressive cycle of what society has deemed appropriate teachings and conditioning.

My new policies, much to my chagrin, were met with discontent and frustration from both teachers and leaders. My office filled with teachers who would come to me with students who were being disciplined and ask, "What would you like me to do?" I had to double down by modeling how to engage with our students. This took away from my other leadership priorities, but this was too important.

I then began to strategically alter the suspension policy. This would be the first of many confrontations with staff about discipline. Despite acknowledging that there would be a plan in place that would be "good for all children," no matter the demographic, I was met with resistance. I marched on, determined to have a school community that would support rather than police. Morris (2016) critiqued that the inequitable and criminal policies affecting girls of color as "much more than a street phenomenon. These policies have seeped into our schools, disrupting one of the most important protective factors in a girl's life: her education" (p. 3). As a result, the expectation of girls of color and their behavior within a school are often in direct conflict with their authenticity.

PUSHBACK FROM STAFF AND FACULTY

Despite my belief that changing the discipline code was the right thing to do, it came a cost. Staff surveys indicated that I was too focused on race in my vision of the school. Some of the teachers would ask if my actions would be the same if I did not lead an urban school with a predominantly girls of color student population. They wondered aloud about my leadership being too color-centric and not color neutral enough (Bonilla-Silva, 2015).

After reading the feedback, I decided to engage my staff in a learning module where they would begin to confront their own issues of race and bias. During a professional development session, I had my teachers read a chapter from Monique W. Morris's book *Pushout* (2016). Morris's book explains that most Black girls are pushed out of schools and into the carceral system. Again, I was surprised by the responses of my staff. Some teachers would criticize the chapter, declaring there were parts of the story being left out. They denied that a young woman of color was targeted for no reason other than her skin color. Cielo's comments came flooding back as I could see their "color blind" stance was blinding them to the reality their students faced. Despite these ridiculous claims, we began to dialogue about issues of race and gender. These conversations were hard for me. I was standing in front of a predominately White faculty, discussing race and equity challenging their notions.

Having faculty who would engage in discussions and action about race to envision and provide a better school environment for our students was of paramount importance to me. It was not enough for me to have teachers that said they wanted to work in the urban setting with girls of color to afford them better opportunities. They had to do the work during the school year in order to support our students in a space that would treat them with the integrity they deserved. By the end of the year, some of the teachers resented the work I had them engage in, while others stated that they appreciated the readings and open dialogue that we had. More than anything, it was clear that the work that began with Cielo's words was work that would need to continue so educators would see the brilliance of the students they served.

REFERENCES

Bonilla-Silva, E. (2015). The structure of racism in color-blind, " Post-racial " America. *American Behavioral Scientist, 59*(11), 1358–1376.

Morris, M. W. (2016). *Pushout: The criminalization of Black girls in schools.* The New Press.

Shange, N. (1974). *for colored girls who have considered suicide/when the rainbow is enuf.* Scribner.

CHAPTER 6

COACHING FOR SUCCESS!

An Administrator's Account About African American Leadership Where All Students Win!

Willie Black, Jr.

The job of public-school educators and administrators has become increasingly challenging. High-stakes achievement tests hold, not only students, but teachers, administrators, and entire school districts accountable for meeting state-mandated educational achievement standards. From the No Child Left Behind Act of 2001, to now Every Student Succeeds Act of 2015 (2019), there is an increased demand for student achievement. In addition, the demographics of the student population are continually changing. For example, by 2025, principals will lead schools where only 46% of the school-aged population will be White, 26% of all children will live in poverty, and 8% will speak a language other than English. Between fall 2013 and fall 2025, the percentages of students enrolled in public schools are projected to continue to decrease for students who are White (from 50 to 46%) and Black (from 16 to 15%). In contrast, the percentages are projected to increase over this period for students who are Hispanic

Purveyors of Change: School Leaders of Color Share Narratives of Student, School, and Community Success, pp. 41–51
Copyright © 2021 by Information Age Publishing
All rights of reproduction in any form reserved.

41

(from 25 to 29%), Asian/Pacific Islander (from 5 to 6%), and of Two or more races (from 3 to 4%). The percentage of students who are American Indian/ Alaska Native is projected to be about 1 percent in 2025 (National Center for Education Statistics [NCES], 2017).

Today's public schools need leadership that is not only culturally sensitive, but also skilled at dealing with the needs of a diverse school population. Yet, many administrators are often not prepared and do not have the skills to meet the challenge (Azzam, 2005). Effective minority school leaders can greatly impact and contribute to school improvement and successful learning for all students (Sanchez et al., 2008). So, how are educators to properly prepare to meet the demands of today's public education system, and what can leaders do to support teachers and students? In this chapter, I will review the current condition of African American leadership, leadership for social justice, transformative leadership qualities, and life coaching and its relevance for educators in public schools.

THE STATE OF AFRICAN AMERICAN LEADERSHIP

African Americans have strongly affirmed the role of education as the key to improving the circumstances in the lives and to promoting social change (Sanchez et al., 2008). In the 19th and early 20th century, African American educators who instructed in private and public institutions held themselves accountable for the education of children and adults who attended their schools (Echols, 2006). During this time, many African American teachers expected every child to succeed and become contributors rather than takers from society.

With the current pressures from Every Student Succeeds Act of 2015 (2019), the standards and expectations for accountability within subpopulations and improved student achievement are clearly present. Accessibility to educational administration relates to having the knowledge of opportunity and belief that there is a possibility to advance to the position. According to Beachum (2004) and Tillman (2004a), knowledge of opportunity has a lot to do with learning about educational administration as a career option and then knowing what skills are needed to take advantage of the opportunity. Effective minority school leaders can positively impact success for all students. According to researchers (Kunjufu, 2006; Lomotey, 1993; Tillman, 2004a), African American principals who serve as role models provide images that inspire and motivate students of color. The means of serving as models also fulfills the principals' role in regard to practicing a form of caring that will in turn empower students to apply alternative social skills in challenging situations, rather than attempting to control student behavior by mere use of authority (Tillman, 2004a). Brown (2005) also emphasized in his work that schools that are racially diverse require leaders and models who address the racial, cultural, and ethnic makeup of the school community. The call to leadership for social justice is a huge undertaking; however, the need for such leaders is imperative to motivate and serve a population that is marginalized in U.S. school systems today.

Schools have increasingly become more ethnically and culturally diverse, but the diversity among school leaders does not reflect the schools' changing demographics (Tillman, 2004a). Whites make up less than one fourth of the student population in the nation's largest cities, while 84% of teachers are White and 75% are female. In P–12 schools nationally, 82% of public-school principals are White, 11% Black, 5% Hispanic, and less than 3% identified as Asian and Native American (NCES, 2017).

LEADERSHIP FOR SOCIAL JUSTICE

There is some variance regarding what makes a good leader and what constitutes effective leadership. According to Bolman and Deal (2003), "Leadership is not a tangible thing. It exists only in relationships and in the imagination and perception of the engaged parties" (p. 337). Some suggest that leaders get things done and get people to do things; leaders are powerful (Shields, 2004). Implicitly, people expect leaders to persuade or inspire rather than to coerce or give orders. Leaders are also expected to produce cooperative effort and pursue goals that go beyond selfish desires. Bogotch (2000) posited that social justice has many meanings, presenting leaders with the ongoing challenge of creating social and political spaces for advocates, both in and out of schools, to explore and make explicit the connections between subjective meanings of social justice.

Social Justice Leadership

In reviewing the literature, there are many definitions of social justice leadership. Goldfarb and Grinberg (2002) defined social justice "as the exercise of altering these [institutional and organizational] arrangements by actively engaging in reclaiming, appropriating, sustaining, and advancing inherent human rights of equity, equality, and fairness in social, economic, educational, and personal dimensions" (p. 162). Social justice leaders, according to Dantley (2002), "will create agendas to deconstruct racism, sexist and ageist epistemological monoliths and will simultaneously construct strategies for resistance and reconstruction" (p. 31). Hoffman (2008) explained such leaders resist, dissent, and are committed to transforming oppressive and exploitative social relations in or out of school.

Theoharis (2007, 2008) has made significant contributions to the field of educational leadership by synthesizing the literature on social justice leadership and developing a conceptual theory of social justice leadership. Theoharis (2007) defined "social justice leadership to mean that these principals make issues of race, class, gender, disability, sexual orientation, and other historically and currently marginalizing conditions in the United stated central to their advocacy, leadership practice, and vision" (p. 223). For purposes of this research, social justice leadership in education is directed towards the principalship. Furthermore, Theoharis's (2007) definition most clearly defines social justice as it relates to the principalship and was used for this study. It is also important to mention that within the scope of this study African American leadership for social justice was the focus; however, all concepts and theories are applicable to leaders who aspire to the position.

African American Leadership for Social Justice

As scholars of color entered into the field of research, attention was heavily focused on communities of color. Larson and Murtadha (2002) argued that these communities were virtually overlooked as sites of inquiry and that uncertainties of academic success and educational achievement for children of color underscore a need for African American leadership.

According to Brown (2005), leadership within African-centered education is a developing field, with a major emphasis on training and mentoring individuals so they can become leaders within this field. Murtadha and Watts (2005) highlighted the history of leaders: "African American leaders formed fraternal orders, literacy groups, and organized church congregations to support collective interests, recognizing that community strengths, not individual abilities, were needed to bring about change" (p. 606). Larson and Murtadha (2002) argued that the inequities in education have been a rallying point for leaders whose skills, defined areas of competence, and stated life purposes are dedicated to achieving greater social justice in education. Moreover, school leaders must be aware of the broader social and political contexts that may be contributing to the students' education (Dantley, 2005a). African-centered educational leaders need to not only stress academic achievement but also the whole development of the students within the current social and political environment (Brown, 2005; Dantley, 2005a). Dantley (2005a) stated,

> Leaders in urban schools especially should engage in serious deliberation with students, teachers, parents, and other community members focused on issues of epistemology and power, self-identity and curriculum, and

pedagogical practices that work to transform curricula, liberate critical thinking, and co-construct knowledge. (p. 653)

African American principals often believe that their communities are at the heart of learning. Lomotey (1989) found that African American principals in successful schools have a sincere confidence in the ability of all African American children to learn, a strong commitment to the education of African American children, and a deep understanding of and compassion for the children and communities they serve. Similarly, Murtadha and Larson (1999) found that the principals in their study viewed community involvement as a critical feature of leadership. These principals developed relationships with their communities and demonstrated a deep compassion for, commitment to, and understanding of the populations they serve. As Black principals working in institutions staffed by a predominantly White staff, they often found themselves standing with their communities and against institutionalized norms that are harmful to Black children.

COMPLEMENTARY LEADERSHIP CHARACTERISTICS

Transformative Leadership

The term *transform* implies major changes in the form, nature, function, and potential of some phenomenon; applied to leadership, it specifies general ends to be pursued, although it is largely mute with respect to means (Leithwood & Prestine, 2002). Leaders are viewed as transformative when they are able to directly influence their followers in terms of the goals and expectations they have for themselves. As the school culture changes, it is imperative that administrators are developed to strongly commit to an ethic of client service (Dantley & Tillman, 2006). Transformative leaders encourage a custom of joint influence that impacts the entire school community (Bass, 1997; Cooper, 2009; Macgregor Burns, 2003). This custom created by the leader fosters a relationship of mutual respect and manifests most directly in shared decision-making about the most significant issues faced by the school and all stakeholders (Leithwood & Jantzi, 1999).

According to Bolman and Deal (2003), "Transforming leaders evoke their constituents' better nature and move them toward higher and more universal needs and purposes. They are visionary leaders whose leadership is inherently symbolic" (p. 361). Transformative leaders help build a common view of their school with their staff regarding their purpose and goals and foster high levels of commitment towards accomplishing these goals and living up to their purpose (Bass, 1997; Cooper, 2009; MacGregor

Burns, 2003). Effective leaders encourage their staff to be open to new ideas and to evaluate new practices critically and with a positive attitude.

Echols (2006) posited that the key to principal success is the perspective that effective leadership is closely entwined with transformative leadership. A definition of social justice that emphasizes the role of the school in social transformation was provided by Dantley and Tillman (2006) as follows:

> The essential components of a definition of social justice include leadership for social justice, moral transformative leadership, and social justice praxis ... which link the principles of democracy and equity in proactive ways so that the social justice agenda becomes a vibrant part of the everyday work of school leaders. (pp. 19–20)

Effective leadership also includes appropriate modeling, intellectual stimulation, evaluation, reevaluation, and reflection (Leithwood & Jantzi, 1999). Although the main mode of operation for principals is that of an instructional leader, Leithwood and Jantzi (1999) argued that this method is no longer sufficient to respond to the challenges that leaders face. Similarly, Obiakor and Beachum (2005) contended that educational leaders have specific roles and relationships to actively engage and promote issues and discourses of race, multiculturalism, and power in schools and other educational settings. Cooper (2009) described transformative leadership engaging in self-reflection; systematically analyzing schools; and then confronting inequities regarding race, class, gender, language, ability, and sexual orientation. Such a leader works toward the social transformation of schooling (Marshall & Oliva, 2006; Theoharis, 2007).

Spiritual Leadership

Spirituality is defined as the part of life through which individuals search for meaning and gain understanding of the world. According to Dantley (2005a), an increase in spiritual leadership is no longer an unmentionable topic, and religion is a subject that can be broached within educational leadership discourse. Dantley posited that educational leaders whose professional practice and leadership is built upon a spiritual foundation clearly understand the multidimensional aspects of their daily challenges and yet find the inner strength to resist hegemonic structures and forms of oppression and systemic inequities in the education system. Dantley (2005b) stated,

> We have reduced education to a contest to determine who can "bank" the most inane facts into students perceived to be empty receptacles. These students are then expected to regurgitate these detached and decontextual-

ized bits of knowledge on vacuous standardized tests whose results are then reported to the public, and erroneous, insubstantial judgments are made about the quality of the educational process. (p. 16)

Schools led by an administrator with a strong sense of morality operate from a position of integrity. Spirituality will afford leaders the opportunity to unashamedly engage in critical reflection, an essential prerequisite to transformation (Dantley, 2002).

Fry (2005) extended spiritual leadership theory by exploring the concept of positive human health and well-being through recent developments in workplace spirituality, character ethics, positive psychology, and spiritual leadership. He then argued that these areas provide a consensus on the values, attitudes, and behaviors necessary for positive human health and well-being. Fry also stated, "Values affect one's perception of the situation or problems, how one relates to others, and act as guides for choices and actions" (p. 54).

Spirituality defines the values and principles that guide individuals' personal lives and professional behavior (Dantley, 2003). It transforms people's lives by enabling them to convert their dreams into real possibilities. Dantley (2003) wrote,

"Purposive leadership" is a description of educational leadership grounded in one of the three tenets West (1988) delineates as part of what he called prophetic spirituality. Purposive leadership, according to Dantley (2003), emanated from what West terms *aggressive pessimism*. Aggressive pessimism, according to West, characterizes the way African Americans have dealt with innumerable obstacles, the plethora of marginalizing structures and rituals that have been systemically embedded in the American societal fabric, as well as the persistent demeaning of their identity due to racist and abrogating acts perpetrated by those persons and institutions representative of the dominant elite. (p. 274)

In recognizing the importance of relationships in leadership, many scholars have suggested that improving education in poor communities requires no longer clinging to objective, role-based images of leadership. Instead, educational leaders must recognize the need to accept responsibility for honest relationships and open communication (Larson & Murtadha, 2002).

LIFE COACHING AND ITS RELEVANCE FOR EDUCATORS

Teachers are people with real lives and issues. More than any other profession, teachers must learn to balance their personal lives, with the challenges

of the school day. How can educators cope with the mounting stress of jug-
gling work and their personal lives? The answer may lie within the practice
of life coaching. The research regarding life coaching for teachers is sparse.
However, a deeper understanding about how it applies to teachers and
the positive effects it can have on student achievement is warranted. Life
coaching might be a valuable approach to help teachers be successful in
their personal lives, and to translate some of these coping skills into their
work, thereby helping them be more effective in the classroom as well.

What Is Life Coaching?

Life coaching is an expert practice which intends to help individuals
flourish throughout everyday life, by living as indicated by their qualities,
endeavoring to achieve objectives, and accomplishing prosperity in all
everyday issues. According to Grant (2003, p. 254) for example: "Life
Coaching can be broadly defined as a collaborative solution-focused,
result-orientated and systematic process in which the coach facilitates the
enhancement of life experience and goal attainment in the personal and/
or professional life of normal, non-clinical clients."

Coaching is distinct from mentoring, therapy, and teaching. Coaching
focuses on working with nonclinical population to achieve specific goals
and work through steps needed to achieve those goals, whereas therapy
focuses on pathology, clinical populations and presenting problems and
diagnoses. A coach-client relationship is viewed as an equal partnership,
however there is an expert-novice relationship in mentoring and teaching
(Lefdahl-Davis et al., 2018). Life coaching is a synergistic relationship
between an accredited life coach and a client designed to tap into your
full potential.

According to Lee (2017), research has shown that conventional preparation and training for educators has limiting effects on raising the instructor
exhibitions inside the classrooms. Because of its individualized approach,
life coaching, then, could have a more impactful effect on teacher performance in the classroom. Various components of life coaching make it a
viable option for supporting teachers with their professional and personal
growth.

Successful Life Coaching Components

- The practice of life coaching must acknowledge and encourage
  what is good in the client and empower them to reach their greatest potential through their greatest strengths.

- Life coaching must occur in a safe and open environment for the client; the coach must create a space where clients feel safe enough to grow.
- Perhaps most important of all, the coach and client must be on equal footing in the relationship, sharing the responsibility for defining and maintaining the coaching relationship.
- Life coaching must be undertaken with a client-centered approach that focuses on the client as an individual with unique needs, strengths, and experience.
- The focus of life coaching must be on the client's whole self, not just specific pieces of the client's personality or in only certain spheres of the client's life.
- As noted earlier, life coaching must be dynamic, as the nature of coaching involves a great deal of change in the client's circumstances, priorities, and needs.

Teaching and leading in public schools today are challenging and sometimes overwhelming tasks. From meeting federal and state standards, to the needs of an ever-changing student population, educators must be adequately prepared both personally and professionally, to deal with the multifaceted demands of their profession. As fewer minority leaders enter the field of education, schools with diverse demographics are largely impacted. Educational leaders of any ethnic background must learn to relate to students different from themselves. It is imperative that principal certification programs seek to purposely prepare educational leaders to operate within culturally diverse school settings. Likewise, services such as life coaching can be beneficial in helping educators grow professionally and personally, in order to be more effective, and in turn, feel more successful within their profession. **Happy Teachers, Happy Students!**

REFERENCES

Azzam, A. M. (2005). The unprepared administrator. *ASCD, 62*(8), 88–89.

Bass, B. M. (1997). Does the transactional-transformational leadership paradigm transcend organizational and national boundaries? *American Psychologist, 52*, 130–139.

Beachum, F. (2004). Black students and middle class teachers [Review of the book *Black students; middle class teachers*, by K. Kunjufu]. *Multicultural Education, 11*(3), 58.

Bolman, L. G., & Deal, T. E. (2003). *Reframing organizations*. Jossey-Bass.

Bogotch, I. E. (2000, April). *Educational leadership and social justice: Theory into practice.* Paper presented at the meeting of the University Council for Educational Administration, Albuquerque, NM.

Cooper, C. W. (2009). Performing cultural work in demographically changing schools: Implications for expanding transformative leadership frameworks. *Educational Administration Quarterly, 45,* 694–724.

Dantley, M. (2002). Uprooting and replacing positivism, the melting pot, multiculturalism, and other important notions in educational leadership through an African American perspective. *Education and Urban Society, 34,* 334–352.

Dantley, M. E. (2003). Purpose-driven leadership: The spiritual imperative to guiding schools beyond high-stakes testing and minimum proficiency. *Education & Urban Society, 35,* 273–291.

Dantley, M. E. (2005a). African American spirituality and Cornel West's notions of prophetic pragmatism: Restructuring educational leadership in American urban schools. *Educational Administration Quarterly, 41,* 651–674.

Dantley, M. E. (2005b). Faith-based leadership: Ancient rhythms or new management. *International Journal of Qualitative Studies in Education, 18*(1), 3–19.

Dantley, M. E., & Tillman, L. C. (2006) Social justice and moral transformative leadership. In C. Marshall & M. Oliva (Eds.), *Leadership for social justice: Making revolutions in education* (pp. 16–30). Pearson.

Echols, C. (2006). *Challenges facing African American principals: A conversation about coping.* Retrieved from the Connexions website: http://cnx.org/content/m13821/1.1/

Every Student Succeeds Act. (2015). (2019). In *Current Events in Context.* Retrieved February 15, 2019. http://www.abc-clio.com/current/

Fry, L. W. (2005). Toward a theory of ethical and spiritual well-being and corporate social responsibility through spiritual leadership. In R. A. Giacalone & C. L. Jurkiewicz (Eds.), *Positive psychology in business ethics and corporate responsibility* (pp. 47–83). Information Age.

Goldfarb, K. P., & Grinberg, J. (2002). Leadership for social justice: Authentic participation in the case of a community center in Caracas, Venezuela. *Journal of School Leadership, 12,* 157–173.

Grant, A. M. (2003). The Impact of Life Coaching on Goal Attainment, Metacognition and Mental Health. *Social Behavior and Personality, 31*(3), 253–264.

Hoffman, D. (2008). *Surviving and thriving as a social justice leader in K–12 education at the "church" of Franklin School: An autoethnography* (Doctoral dissertation). Retrieved from ProQuest Dissertations and Theses database. (UMI 3314323)

Kunjufu, J. (2006). *An African centered response to Ruby Payne's poverty theory.* African American Images

Lefdahl-Davis, E. M., Huffman, L., Stancil, J., & Alayan, A. J. (2018). The impact of life coaching on undergraduate students: A multiyear analysis of coaching outcomes. *International Journal of Evidence Based Coaching and Mentoring, 16*(2), 69–83.

Larson, C., & Murtadha, K. (2002). *Leadership for social justice.* University of Chicago Press.

Lee, J. (2017). 'We can't do it just to make them feel good': An exploration into the benefits of coaching in secondary schools. *International Coaching Psychology Review*, *12*, 110–124.

Leithwood, K., & Jantzi, D. (1999). The relative effects of principal and teacher sources of leadership on student engagement with school. *Educational Administration Quarterly*, *35*, 679–706.

Leithwood, K., & Prestine, N. (2002). Unpacking the challenges of leadership at the school and district level. *Yearbook of the National Society for the Study of Education, 101*(1), 42–64.

Lomotey, K. (1989). *African-American principals: School leadership and success.* Greenwood.

Lomotey, K. (1993). African-American principals. *Urban Education, 27*, 395–412. https://doi.org/10.1177/0042085993027004005

MacGregor Burns, J. (2003). *Transforming Leadership: A New Pursuit of Happiness.* Grove Press.

Marshall, C., & Oliva, M. (2006). *Leaders for social justice: Making revolutions in education.* Allyn & Bacon.

Murtadha, K., & Larson, C. (1999, April). *Toward a socially critical, womanist theory of leadership.* Paper presented at the meeting of the American Educational Research Association, Montreal, Quebec, Canada.

Murtadha, K., & Watts, D. M. (2005). Linking the Struggle for Education and Social Justice: Historical Perspectives of African American Leadership in Schools. *Educational Administration Quarterly, 41*(4), 591–608. https://doi.org/10.1177/0013161X04274271

National Center for Education Statistics. (2017). *Digest of education statistics 2017.*

No Child Left Behind Act of 2001, Pub. L. No. 107-110 (2002).

Obiakor, F. E., & Beachum, F. D. (2005). Developing self-empowerment in African American students using the Comprehensive Support Model. *Journal of Negro Education, 74*(1), 18–29. Retrieved from http://search.ebscohost.com.tamusa.idm.oclc.org/login.aspx?direct=true&db=a9h&AN=17224663&site=ehost-live&scope=site

Sanchez, J., Thornton, B., & Usinger, J. (2008). *Promoting diversity in public education leadership.* Retrieved from the Connexions Web site: http://cnx.org/content/m18745/1.2/

Shields, C. M. (2004). Dialogic leadership for social justice: Overcoming pathologies of silence. *Educational Administration Quarterly, 40*, 109–132.

Theoharis, G. (2007). Social justice educational leaders and resistance: Toward a theory of social justice leadership. *Educational Administration Quarterly, 43*, 221–258.

Theoharis, G. (2008). Woven in deeply: Identity and leadership of urban social justice principals. *Education and Urban Society, 41*, 3–25.

Tillman, L. C. (2004a). African American principals and the legacy of *Brown*. *Review of Research in Education, 28*, 101–146.

CHAPTER 7

PLANNING FOR STUDENT SUCCESS

Addressing Academic Achievement and Social Emotional Well-Being

Renee L. Garraway

"We are not in a position in which we have nothing to work with. We already have capacities, talents, direction, missions, callings."

—Abraham Maslow

I remember slipping into my imaginary world to escape the emotional pain I felt from being in a classroom where the teacher made it obvious that she did not care for children of color. Some of the other children in my first-grade classroom recognized that they could also get away with being mean to me and I endured unkind verbal attacks from my classmates who were predominantly White or lighter complexioned Blacks. In the early 1970s, I do not recall seeing images of beautiful Black people in my schoolbooks, on television, or even in my neighborhood. The only pictures I saw of Black people were those in my outdated social studies book, who were covered in

Purveyors of Change: School Leaders of Color Share Narratives of Student, School, and Community Success, pp. 53–61
Copyright © 2021 by Information Age Publishing

mud, wearing grass skirts with spheres in hand. In my home, we did not talk about Black pride and I had no positive role models to encourage me and make me feel that I was just as good as the little White girls in my class. I felt lonely and invisible, not only at school, but in my neighborhood where my dad and two sisters seemed to be favored because of their light complexion.

By the time I reached third grade, I met one of my most remarkable teachers and mentor, Ms. Thompson. Ms. Thompson, a sophisticated Black woman, was a strict, no-nonsense teacher who demanded respect from her students. She was one of the few teachers who took an interest in me, encouraged me, and asked me questions to ensure that I understood and could succeed. Although I was often nervous about being called on in her class, I knew she cared about me, and for the very first time, I felt I belonged in school. After my completion of third grade, the pressures of home-life combined with school stressors (lack of relevant instruction, discrimination, and bullying) began to haunt me again. My fourth-grade teacher rarely said anything to me, and I was once again an invisible learner who yearned to feel connected to my teacher, classmates, and the learning environment. Since I was rarely asked to share my thoughts and had very limited opportunities to engage in meaningful discourse, I often felt bored and found myself escaping the classroom by daydreaming. I learned to memorize and regurgitate information in order to obtain good grades. Rarely did my teachers help me to make real-word connections to what I was learning and rarely was I asked if I understood the content being taught. By the time I got to middle school, I felt defeated and suffered from low self-esteem.

After relocating to Michigan to finish high school, I started to realize that I had gaps in my learning. My Aunt Sarah and Uncle Rohlann instilled in me the value of education and insisted that I study even when I had no homework. They believed in me and helped me to realize my self-worth and potential for greatness. My move was the "resurrection" I needed in order to see a clearer path to success. Although I failed the ninth grade, with the support of my family, I took summer and night classes to get back on track. I attended Samuel C. Mumford High School, a predominantly Black high school, where I met teachers who genuinely cared about me and offered support outside of class when needed. During my junior year, I was able to achieve honor roll status which gave me a thirst for more learning and success. Uncle Rohlann held me accountable for my learning by asking me a series of questions when I came home each day to ensure that I understood what I learned and why it was important. My uncle and aunt are responsible for helping me to see my potential, excel in college, and giving me hope for a productive future. To this day, Uncle Rohlann still asks me thought provoking questions to check my understanding!

After high school graduation, I was very excited to get accepted to a small university in Michigan. My uncle thought education would be a good fit and encouraged me to make the selection as my major. I had no idea what I wanted to major in, but knew I was not smart enough or confident enough to be anybody's teacher! When I reflect on my hesitation to major in education, I realize that some of my school experiences impacted my confidence in teachers and my self-esteem. Most of my primary school experience was devastating not only because of the racism by my teachers and bullying by peers, but as a result of mediocre teaching. Instead of selecting education as a major, I completed a career inventory and decided on psychology. I had a rough start in college until I realized that I actually had to study if I wanted to stay! The hard work paid off and four years later, I was blessed to receive an academic scholarship for a master's degree from The University of Michigan School of Social Work. A few years later I received another scholarship to The George Washington University for a master's degree in special education. I never anticipated that I would become an educator, let alone an assistant principal, because of my negative school experiences and lack of confidence. I often share my story with my students in an effort to demonstrate that perseverance, in spite of roadblocks, can lead to success. I also find that sharing my story with my staff helps to shine a light on the unlocked potential of our students. Furthermore, I hope that sharing my story helps my staff understand the necessity of building positive relationships with students and creating a learning environment so that they can maximize their potential.

IDENTIFYING PURPOSE

As an educational leader, my purpose is to advocate for marginalized youth of color to ensure that they receive rigorous, engaging, and relevant learning opportunities in a safe and nurturing learning environment. As an assistant principal, I served as a champion for youth placed "at-risk." I made it clear to my staff that as a school family we would engage and support students and meet not only their academic, but social-emotional needs. For instance, one of my most challenging students, Nia (pseudonym), was constantly in trouble at school and in the community. Her attendance was poor and when she did come to school she was disruptive and disengaged. Nia enjoyed coming to my office, but as an administrator, I also wanted her to connect with other staff, especially her classroom teachers. Staff had difficulty working with Nia because some of them did not take the time to build a relationship with her. As I reflect on Nia's experience, she, like many other students of color, may have felt invisible in an environment that should have been more welcoming and supportive. Nia's pain turned into anger and she did not hold back when using profanity to express her feelings towards staff. Many staff expressed relief when she was not in school instead of considering the barriers that impacted her availability for instruction. Several unsuccessful phone calls and home visits led us to seek outside referrals. The turning point occurred when Nia arrived at school in crisis mode and required intensive community support. During the intake meeting, Nia was assigned a mentor, someone who also connected well with her mother. Once the mentor helped to foster a positive relationship with the family, Nia became more trusting of our staff. Doing this gave Nia hope for her future and in turn, her attendance and grades improved. Nia called a few years ago to inform me that she had a child, was employed, and living independently. She thanked me for the time I took to visit her home years prior and said that she would always consider me family. At that moment, I felt relieved-a sense of peace, a sense of purpose.

COMMUNICATING BELIEFS AND VALUES

My professional and personal experiences impact my passion for closing the achievement gap and ensuring that all students, especially students of color, are successful. In my work as an educational leader, I have found that sharing my core values has positively influenced relationships with students and families:

- Building positive relationships with stakeholders
- Effectively communicate (respect and transparency)
- Collaborate with invested stakeholders to address barriers to student success (see Figure 7.1).

Educational leaders should feel empowered to set the tone for a climate that honors multicultural diversity and is inclusive of all stakeholders (Gallagher, 2012; Irvine, 2012). All invested stakeholders bring unique experiences, talents, and skills that can be utilized to positively impact the lives of students. As an educational leader, I want to be known for building positive relationships and collaborating with all invested stakeholders to positively impact the lives of all students and to ensure that students have the academic and social skills needed to lead productive lives. To truly meet students' academic and social-emotional needs, educators needed to strive to become culturally proficient (Gay, 2010; Ladson-Billings, 2009). Cultural proficiency is an ongoing learning experience (Gay, 2010). It first takes self-reflection and an open mind to engage with others of diverse cultures and backgrounds and to seek understanding. I continuously strive to become a culturally proficient leader. Some of the steps I have taken with my school team to move us towards reflection, identification of biases, and improved practice include:

Figure 7.1

Core Values

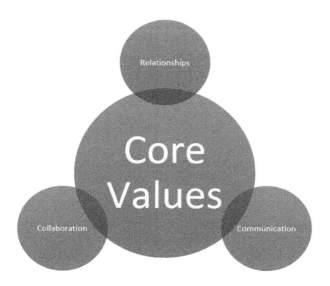

- Frequent (focus) student observations, feedback, and data chats in an effort to close the achievement gap.
- Examining student work to determine student needs/differentiation.
- Analyze data, drill-down to racial and special education subgroups, identify gaps, create a school-wide cultural proficiency plan, and encourage each team to create a team plan.
- Collaborate with the Parents' Diversity Council (e.g., local NAACP) in an effort to build and support a stronger network of resources for the goal of quality education and well-roundedness for all children, particularly diverse minority children.
- Serve as a member of the Parent Teacher Associations' Board to educate and collaborate with parents on issues of equity to continue the work of closing the achievement gap and ensuring success for all students.
- Register with staff to take professional development courses through the Equity Initiatives Unit to deepen our understanding of culturally and linguistically diverse students.
- Read empirical literature related to culturally responsive educational leadership in an effort to enhance leadership practice.

Schools desiring to improve the academic and social-emotional well-being of their students will need to become more comfortable in having ongoing conversations about race and equity and acknowledge that their beliefs and practices impact student achievement. This means that some educators will be uncomfortable, but the opportunities for self-reflection and examining beliefs can be a powerful first step in informing practice.

PLANNING FOR SUCCESS

In order to meet the needs of all students, I engage invested stakeholders in conversations about what students need to experience success. For instance, during collaborative team planning meetings (DuFour, 2011) we examine the curriculum and create a plan to ensure that lessons are engaging and that all learners can make sense of challenging content. These conversations may also revolve around getting to know the students they teach and helping students make connections with the curriculum for meaningful and lifelong learning experiences (Gay, 2010; Ladson-Billings, 2009). Our team panning also consists of discussions about difficult to engage students and how to teach and model positive social skills for life –long success. During classroom visits, I found that documenting equitable practices and sharing with the staff at meetings served as a motivator and learning experience for others.

To further provide opportunities for professional development on cultural competency, we partnered with a local university to facilitate inquiry groups focused on the overrepresentation of Black males in office referrals. We analyzed discipline data, determined key themes and areas of focus (i.e., developed a plan). All of the staff who participated in the inquiry groups reported that they were more intentional in building relationships with students and engaged in meaningful equitable practices (i.e., greeting each student at the door in the morning; making positive calls home; having lunch with students, etc.). During school-wide staff meetings, our agendas included ongoing conversations about equitable practices to improve student achievement and support their social-emotional development. When student data were analyzed during weekly grade level team meetings, a discussion of gap students (lower performers) and students needing enriched instruction was expected. Our team level meeting discussions included:

- Mastery objectives (team consistency to ensure student success)
- Content specific vocabulary (especially supports non-English speakers)
- Possible barriers or areas of confusion for students
- Strategies FOR DIFFERENTIATION TO ADDRESS BARRIERS

CONSIDERATIONS FOR CULTURALLY RESPONSIVE
EDUCATIONAL LEADERS

Visibility and Engagement

Visibility and engagement have proven to be effective means of collecting informal data. For years, I have used a classroom visit log and scheduled time on my Outlook calendar to ensure that I make the time to consistently observe teaching and learning. Visiting several classrooms per day to monitor instruction is a practice I have found that provides greater insight into teaching and learning needs. The practice of visiting classrooms daily and providing timely feedback to teachers can prevent unnecessary problems. In addition, the use of a student observation document to collect data on gap/focus students can serve as a valuable tool. The aforementioned documents can be used for teacher feedback, growth, and reflection.

Analyzing Data to Inform Practice

At least once per month, I visit each grade level's collaborative team planning meetings and data chats. During collaborative team planning meetings, I work with teams to consistently analyze student data, discuss instructional practices, and identify resources to support teaching and learning in an effort to improve outcomes for focus students. As an instructional leader, I strive to ensure that all staff members have a repertoire of strategies to enhance their teaching practice and the necessary resources so that all students can fully access the curriculum.

Nurturing Learning Environment

As a clinical social worker, special educator, and school-based administrator, I understand the importance of building positive relationships with staff and students in order to ensure a productive learning environment. Consistently making positive connections, modeling respect, and talking to staff and students about what they need in order to experience success has been effective in improving teacher practice and student performance. The practice of intentionally building positive relationships with staff, students, and parents is critical to ensuring that all students have what they need to experience success in a safe and nurturing learning environment (see Figure 7.2).

In order to close the achievement gap, school leaders need to work collaboratively with all invested stakeholders to ensure that every staff member has opportunities and resources necessary to meet the needs

Figure 7.2

Academic and Social-Emotional Well-Being

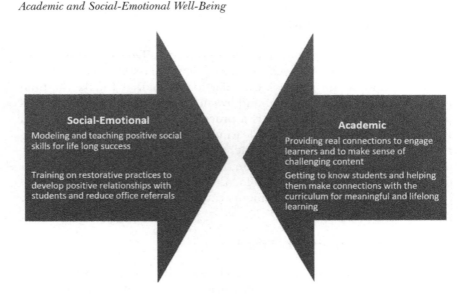

of all learners. Doing this will mean that more students can walk out of the school building with hope and the skills necessary to have a productive future. If teachers provide rigorous, engaging, and relevant learning opportunities and check students' understanding, then students will be more engaged in their learning and will experience academic success. In addition, it is imperative that students receive instruction in a safe and nurturing learning environment so that they will remain present and engaged in school. Both culturally responsive teaching practices (Ladson-Billings; Gaye, 2010) and social-emotional learning produce improved academic performance (Gallagher, 2012; Garraway, 2017). When we keep this in mind, we can begin to close the achievement gap.

REFERENCES

DuFour, R., & Marzaon, R. (2011). *Leaders of learning: How district, school, and classroom leaders improve student achievement.* Solution Tree Press.

Gallagher, K. S. (Ed.). (2012). *Urban Education: A model for leadership and policy.* Routledge.

Garraway, R. L. (2017). Transitioning to kindergarten: Improving outcomes for preschool children with behavioral challenges. In A. L. Ellis (Ed.), *Transitioning children with disabilities: From early childhood through adulthood* (pp. 113–128). Sense.

Gay, G. (2010). *Culturally responsive teaching: Theory, research, and practice*. Teachers College Press.

Ladson-Billings, G. (2009). *The dream-keepers: Successful teachers of African American children*. Jossey-Bass.

Irvine, J. J. (2012). Complex relationships between multicultural education and special education: An African American perspective. *Journal of Teacher Education, 63*(4), 268–274.

CHAPTER 8

DISTRICT-LEVEL PROGRAMS FOR BLACK STUDENT SUCCESS

Constraints and Opportunities for Leaders, Staff, and Community

Wil Greer

As a school district program specialist, I had an opportunity to work on two projects that had critical implications for Black children. The first was the ASHANTI program (a pseudonym). ASHANTI was started in the 2005–2006 academic year and was borne out of a pressing desire to improve the academic achievement and disproportionate discipline rates of Black students. Meetings with site, district, and community leaders, parents, and teachers led to the same conclusions stated in the relevant literature—that the issues underlying the opportunity gaps faced by Black children were multivariate, and that for teachers to be effective with them they needed additional skills and dispositions. In part, they needed to be culturally responsive.

Thereafter, ASHANTI was designed to better meet the instructional, relational, social, and psychological needs of a select group of Black

Purveyors of Change: School Leaders of Color Share Narratives of Student, School, and Community Success, pp. 63–69
Copyright © 2021 by Information Age Publishing

students in the district. There were two school sites that were interested in and able to pilot the program. This was because they had (a) highly supportive principals, (b) some motivated teachers with culturally responsive skill sets, and (c) Black student populations that were large enough to create full ASHANTI classes. These schools were on the district's west side. One was an elementary school and the other was their feeder middle school. They would end up being the only schools to ever offer the program.

Though the program did not discriminate, and the classes had students of all ethnicities, ASHANTI was the first major district initiative designed to address issues faced by students of color. By 2007 the district launched a new office, the Department of Multicultural Student Success (DMSS—a pseudonym). Except for some computers and SMART boards, ASHANTI was not funded by the district office. The DMSS, however, was given some full-time staff who provided training and support to ASHANTI teachers and others. I was the first program specialist in this department, and we had one director, and one secretary. As an aside, I truly relished this role. Coming out of the classroom, it not only gave me my first opportunities to design and deliver professional development, and to coach teachers, but there was a tremendous sense of purpose and pride. Our department's aim was to directly improve outcomes for Black students. We voraciously studied the literature, attended conferences, and were zealous about improving the district so it could better support our children.

And to some degree, this happened. The ASHANTI teachers were among the best in the district. They were highly adept at creating positive and affirming classrooms, using culturally responsive curricular materials, teaching to students' unique learning styles, eliciting varied types of student responses, designing collaborative and interactive learning experiences, ensuring students used academic vocabulary, and teaching higher order thinking in context. Moreover, they were extremely caring, loving, patient, and innovative in the classroom.

At the same time, they were demanding and never subjected the kids to the soft bigotry of low expectations. I would walk into ASHANTI classrooms and routinely see the students in the middle of an intense debate about a passage they had read in a text that was above their grade level, or about whether their teacher had accurately identified the diameter, radius, and circumference of a circle (she often would not, then dare students to show her how she had gotten it wrong, much to their delight). They were regularly learning on their feet, playing class games, giving performances and presentations, working outside, studying in small groups, or using technology. And they were always accountable to each other, and to their teachers, for their learning. Adorning the walls were pictures of notable Black figures, the principles of Ma'at and Kwanzaa, HBCU pennants and banners, students' families, and their recently graded assignments.

Today, however, the ASHANTI program is in limbo—it neither officially exists, nor was it ever terminated. Its presence has always depended on a coalition of willing site principals, teachers, and DMSS support providers. The middle school that once offered it no longer does so, and its principal left the site long ago. The same is true of the elementary school that provided ASHANTI, though their new principal is interested in continuing the program, and there are two teachers who are attempting to do so. Though we provided culturally responsive teaching workshops to hundreds of teachers and administrators through DMSS, we never effectively grew the ASHANTI program. And outside of the federal and state mandates for collecting disaggregated data by ethnicity, we did not make a concerted district-wide push for equitable outcomes by race.

Consequently, not much data has been collected and maintained for ASHANTI. Almost none of its founding administrators, teachers, or support providers currently work in the district, and maintaining it is not technically the responsibility of any department or person. Though DMSS has always supported the program, it is an office with four full time staff. They must work effectively in one of the largest districts in the state and several dozen schools. Given staffing and budget limitations, and district priorities, they are rethinking the scale and scope of ASHANTI.

As a result, there is perhaps no written or published evidence which attests to the program's effectiveness, nor is much known of the students who once sat in its classrooms. A few years of state, district, and classroom data have been maintained by this writer, as well as some former teachers. Those data show that ASHANTI students often performed better than their school and district peers in math and English. Still, a number of unanswered questions remain. For instance:

1. What impact did the ASHANTI program have on the reading and math performance of Black students?
2. What impact did it have on student discipline rates?
3. If it was successful, what skills and dispositions did ASHANTI teachers have, and how can they be replicated?
4. How many former ASHANTI students went on to, or have graduated from college?
5. Of those who did, to what extent did ASHANTI help them in their journey?
6. If former students believe ASHANTI was helpful, in what ways did it help them succeed in school and in life?

The challenges posed by a lack of formal data presents some key opportunities to current district administrators as well as to researchers. A qualitative program evaluation or impact study would be especially valuable. It could help identify what worked and help with thinking through the challenges of replication. Given the limited data on former ASHANTI student success, interviews with past students and document analysis would (a) enable investigators to learn more about the program through different lenses, and (b) it could provide credible data if the sample size of former students is small. Snowball sampling techniques would provide a sensible approach for beginning data collection. Document analysis could help triangulate the interview data. Documents might include board and district policies regarding DMSS and ASHANTI, any relevant memoranda from district or site administrators, relevant memoranda between ASHANTI teachers and administrators, details of supporting budgets, photos of classrooms, student work samples, and correspondence from students and families.

At any rate, a formal assessment of the ASHANTI program should be undertaken for several reasons. For one, issues of Black student achievement and disproportionate discipline continue to warrant investigation, critical thought, and strategic planning. Unfortunately, it is still the case today, as it was in 2005 when ASHANTI was started, that Black children have the largest opportunity gaps in math and English when the data are disaggregated by ethnicity, and are negatively disciplined at rates of two to three times their other ethnic peers. If ASHANTI was curbing or even reversing these trends, this should be known, along with the mechanisms by which these results occurred. Moreover, the data might support the repositioning or promoting of former ASHANTI teachers. If they were especially effective, there may be more crucial roles for them to play in new teacher induction, onboarding, mentoring, and coaching. They may also excel as administrators with teacher recruitment, hiring, evaluation, retention, and in human resources.

THE HONORS PROJECT

Another venture with significant implications for Black students was the Honors Project (a pseudonym—HP). The Honors Project was an extremely intriguing idea that sought to get more Black high school students into honors and advanced placement (AP) courses. It was the result of a series of DMSS conversations and investigations into district student achievement data. Though there were persistent opportunity gaps between Black students and their peers, it was also true that many Black students were successful, especially at the elementary and middle school levels. However, when we examined high school course enrollments there appeared to be a pattern wherein most of the successful Black students, especially males, were in the least rigorous programs and courses.

Over the course of a few months we studied longitudinal data on the nearly 3,000 Black high school students in our district. For each student, we examined their previous three years of state test scores, grade point averages (GPAs), and special program placement. We excluded students who were already in advanced courses or enrolled in continuation school, where advanced courses were not offered. We also examined the individual cases of students receiving special education services. We hypothesized that anyone who averaged a 3.0 GPA or above over the previous three years (sixth, seventh, and eighth grade), *and* was proficient or advanced on the state math or English test for at least two of those three years, could probably participate in an advanced course.

With these criteria in place we set out to identify students who were not in honors or advanced courses but could be. And thus, the HP was born. After months of analyzing data and checking student records, we identified roughly 600 prospective HP students. Again, these were students who seemed to have the aptitude for honors and AP courses, but simply had not been enrolled in them. They attended every comprehensive high school in our district. We met with each of the high school principals to notify them of our findings. We spoke with various district leaders and support providers as well. Initially, everyone seemed supportive. Yet, one idea that came out of these early meetings—an idea we had admittedly overlooked and never fully investigated—was that the HP students would need some additional level of support if they were going to be successful in more challenging courses. It would not be enough, we agreed, to simply enroll 600 Black students in advanced placement classes and hope for the best. At the very least they would need some combination of mentoring, tutoring, additional counseling, and student success services.

As that conversation was brewing, we eagerly (and unwisely) pushed ahead. We had address labels printed for each HP student and we sent their parents a letter that described the program. We explained how the students were identified, and how taking advanced courses could help them in the future. We also invited their families to community meetings we set up at each high school. Hoping that the HP might just have a hand in helping 600 more Black students succeed in school, receive rigorous instruction, and matriculate to college, we felt enormously excited and optimistic. Unfortunately, this enthusiasm was misguided, and was not based on a strong foundation.

For one, the student support issues mentioned above were never resolved. It would be fair to say that each principal we met with shared our enthusiasm for seeing more Black kids in AP courses. However, they also saw what we could not as district program specialists. They shared concerns about whether all of their AP teachers would be as enthusiastic to see an entirely new crop of students in their classes, and whether every teacher was skilled and prepared enough to accommodate students who were unfamiliar with AP culture and rigor. More pointedly, some questioned whether their teachers were culturally responsive enough to meet the needs of a large influx of Black students.

This last concern was especially palpable. Through DMSS we provided culturally responsive teacher training for district teachers and leaders. However, it was not mandatory, and we failed to develop a customized set of trainings specifically for honors and AP teachers. Though the College Board has been providing its annual *A Dream Deferred* conference to create equity in AP since 2005, there were unanswered questions about who would pay for teachers to go. These were real challenges with no simple solutions.

Another issue that hampered the success of HP was that it was not very popular with students and parents. Many in the student focus groups we met with felt that honors and AP courses were unnecessary, would isolate them from their friends or favorite teachers, and that they might be more challenging than what they had grown accustomed to. Parents, conversely, took more of a *wait and see* approach, which likely indicated a blend of suspicion for the district and hope that we would actually help their children. Consequently, they did not immediately show high interest, but they also were not opposed to their children taking the courses. Indeed, most parents were thrilled that their students had been identified as having potential for an advanced program. However, they often deferred to their children, and allowed them to decide whether they would participate, stay in the courses, or withdraw.

Withdraw they did. That following year—the first and only year the HP was attempted—masses of students dropped their advanced courses; many did so within the first few weeks of school. This outcome was almost predictable, as the previously discussed supports, such as mentoring, tutoring, additional counseling, and student success services, were never provided. The principals had legitimate questions about the supports and did not commit to paying for or organizing them. Meanwhile, the DMSS operated on what amounted to a shoestring budget and did not have the funds to cover much more than its staffing costs. Unfortunately, the tab was never picked up, or even seriously considered, by any other school district department or leader.

In the end, the HP did not turn out to be a far-reaching, well-coordinated project that impacted the lives of hundreds of Black kids. It was, however, an equity-focused and data-driven idea with implications for current district leaders. Any district where leaders are serious about improving access and equity in gifted, honors, or AP programs can engage in a similar analysis of data, based on similar or locally-determined criteria. However, analyzing the data is the easy part. The challenge, as we discovered, is in the coordination of people, spirits, and budgets. In retrospect, we launched the program too soon, were not as people-focused as we should have been, and we came to the table with too few resources.

Going forward, a better strategy might be to apply for and secure grant dollars before attempting implementation. Then, an entire one to two years before implementation, an implementation team should meet frequently to plan for the stages, challenges, and drivers of change. During this period of exploration, the team should work out issues such as who will teach the courses, how and by whom they will be trained, how students will be supported (e.g., counseling, mentoring, tutoring), how teachers will be supported (e.g., coaching, ongoing professional development, professional collaboration), possible benchmarks for student success, and program evaluation. After resolving these issues and coordinating a well-organized plan, only then should children be exposed to the new structure. In short, this work must be approached in a more collaborative, systematic, and thoughtful manner, and it must take the complexities of such change into consideration. By doing so our students will have a better shot at thriving in advanced courses and meeting their full academic potential.

PART III

RESILIENCE, PERSISTENCE, AND TURNAROUND

CHAPTER 9

THE NEGLIGENCE OF CONFORMIST LEADERSHIP

Joseph N. Cerna

Current publicity regarding America's public schools suggests an imperative need for change in practice based on academic achievement results. Curiously, the idea of school reform is not a result of contemporary research. Initially, public schools were established to protect the economic status and power of the elite through hegemonic systems (Freire 2010; Spring 2011). Unfortunately, some educators champion education as the "Golden Ticket" to a better life free from subtle and overt oppressive influences. K–12 student performance on state assessments in stated such as Texas is simplistically used as a projection of success in higher education or in their choice career path including the military. In other words, an 8-year old's reading and math performance on the end of year state assessment is believed to credibly project their future without acknowledgement of the many variables each child faces or might encounter as they navigate a public-school system void of cultural awareness.

The current paternalistic, tiered system of education has existed from the outset. The wealthy had access to political and economic resources to maintain their status while those lacking social capital struggled with limited opportunities for social mobility by design. The accumulation of

Purveyors of Change: School Leaders of Color Share Narratives of Student, School, and Community Success, pp. 73–83
Copyright © 2021 by Information Age Publishing
All rights of reproduction in any form reserved.

73

resources, such as space, reinforced this system of inequality and oppression. The economically disadvantaged were kept separated from elites in areas of political, economic and class influence such as public education and housing. Access to space becomes an outcome of economic power (Morgan, 2000). As a result, lower classes are forced to attend low performing schools that are heavily influenced by elite agendas. These agendas systematically discredit the diverse culture, languages and institutions found in many economically disadvantaged areas.

The number of stakeholders influencing educational reform has grown to include political, economic and assessment agencies. Federal and state government agencies overtly promote the dominant belief system into the educational system under the guise of advocacy for the elimination of inequality and oppression. By standardizing the curriculum and testing, these entities influence the subject matter presented to the masses of students enrolled in public schools (Gabbard, 2008). By controlling the present, the dominant class unilaterally controls the past and influences the future.

Federal and state agencies develop ideologies that present well and foundationally serve all members of society in theory. In Texas, struggling campuses, based on state assessment data, are provided with support and funding. These priority campuses are required to consult with state agency appointed service providers to evaluate needs, current programs, and influence budgeting. The campus organizational chart, unwillingly, includes a state appointed service provider at the decision level to which the site-based leadership team and principal must consult advisement as was the case in two of the campuses I served as principal. If the campus fails to meet state academic performance goals in consecutive years, the level of involvement increases. Federal sanctions are also introduced to the campus and include models of improvement that range from change in leadership to school closure. These models include the Transformation model which suggests replacing the principal and implementing new governance. The Turnaround model replaces the principal and rehiring no more than half of the school staff. The Restart model involves closing and reopening the school under the management of an effective charter operator, charter management organization, or education management organization. The school closure model literally requires the school to close sending students to other, higher-performing schools in the district. Additionally, stated that adopt common, state-developed, college- and career-ready standards are given priority for federal funding.

Threatened with these types of sanctions, many schools seek a K–12 curricula that are increasingly more standardized and heavily influenced by publishers affiliated with state assessments that stand to benefit economically by providing intervention programs. Traditional stakeholders such as parents, community members, site-based leadership teams, campus administrators, students, and teachers have unknowingly deferred their power to federal and state agencies as a result of poor assessment data.

Campus leaders are now considered successful if they can meet state and federal minimum standards. The perception of the campus by stakeholders, however, is stained by the overemphasis on state assessment data by faculty and staff and lack of student-centered learning activities and community pride. I suggest that effective and courageous leadership can yield greater outcomes by emphasizing cultural awareness, defying the pedagogical conformity of leadership preparation programs, making connections through shared experiences, and acknowledging their own professional and cultural leadership duality.

CULTURAL AWARENESS

As a leader in the K–12 educational system for nearly two decades, I realize how the pressure of external forces, with little to no experience in the K–12 educational system, forces district leadership to behave in a manner that is in direct conflict with the district's stated mission and vision. This duplicity results in campus leaders to either clutch their career aspirations through morally justified compliance or to truly advocate for the marginalized populations they vowed to serve by taking great risks. These conformist leaders believe that students simply need to meet the measures of success defined and assessed by legislators to successfully navigate the K–12 system of public education overtly neglecting students' diversity and cultural assets.

Measures of success, such as college readiness, are evaluated by norm-referenced assessments, which more accurately indicate socioeconomic status than aptitude. These measures of success redirect failure to the local level of implementation to which campus leaders respond by focusing efforts on improving state assessment achievement at the minimum level of performance to avoid state agency sanctions or demotion. The root of the disparity, however, is grossly neglected as campus and district leaders' positions are threatened by demotion or termination. In my assignment as a principal in an urban school district, I was explicitly told that if our campus did not meet state minimum standards by the end of the school year I would be reassigned to a demoted position. This directive came with a pseudo-legal agreement document for me to sign. When I questioned the document's legality, it was explained to me that by not signing I was agreeing to a more immediate reassignment. As a second-year principal, I firmly believed that our district leadership neglected the root of our limited academic progress. I quickly realized that my approach to student success conflicted with our district leaders' approach. I believed that academic success was the outcome accentuating the strengths of the campus community not daily state assessment drills. Despite the threat of reassignment and demotion, I worked to establish a culture of student and campus pride developed around community strengths. Strengths included pride in community, creative expression through faith based and cultural art, dance, and song. After our fifth year, we not only met state minimum standards, but also performed in the top 25% of the state based on student progress. These outcomes reinforced my belief that although academic achievement primarily contributes to the federal and state systems of accountability, the most effective leader for campuses serving traditionally marginalized populations requires more than curriculum and instruction expertise.

The most effective leader for the types of campuses discussed possesses unique qualities that might not be taught in traditional leadership preparation programs but could be acquired through direct meaningful experiences. The qualities relevant to transforming these types of campuses are cultural awareness, shared experiences with those served and familiarity with the concept of professional and cultural leadership duality. This is not to suggest that only individuals with congruent backgrounds with the campus community can transform a campus, but instead suggests that the leader should adapt to the community before attempting to influence significant curriculum change. Though the risk is great with this approach, the outcomes are aligned the tenants of social justice and can be sustained over time.

DEFYING PEDAGOGICAL CONFORMITY OF LEADERSHIP PREPARATION PROGRAMS

Educators are traditionally trained in pedagogical theory but lack knowledge and experience in working with students of underserved populations (Bloom & Owens, 2011). This raises questions about the educational equity provided as many teachers may not have adequate knowledge or awareness of how to work with diverse groups of students and may unknowingly perpetuate the achievement gap (Howard, 2010; Valenzuela, 1999).

Cultural differences should be included when developing educational practices and curricula while combating structural discrimination to address the achievement gap (Hernandez & Kose, 2010). At the same time, identifying and recognizing cultural differences should not be a means for campuses to excuse themselves from inequities or gaps in achievement (Brown et al., 2010). Hernandez and Kose (2010) also remind leaders that closing the achievement gap is not as simple as picking up math scores, instead students and staff must remain cognizant of their own culture to stay connected to their identity while improving academic performance. In an ideal educational system, all campus leaders have the ability to develop campus specific plans for improvement beyond core content. Bloom and Owens (2011) found that leaders in low achieving urban schools had influence in school funding while leaders in high achieving urban schools had more influence in hiring, firing and curriculum issues. This finding suggests that effective change is difficult for leaders in low achieving schools as leaders are limited in the areas they influence. Campus measures of effectiveness and subsequent school reform efforts rely heavily on standardized tests (Bloom & Owens, 2011). These indicators fail to acknowledge social and geographic disparities across the nation, state, or city. Issues such as poverty, discrimination based on race and economic status, and teachers lacking training in appropriate pedagogy necessary to teach children from underserved populations are not represented on current quantifiable data (Bloom & Owens, 2011).

As a result, campuses with the largest achievement gaps are forced to implement board adopted intervention programs and subject to strict state monitoring. Furthermore, a significant percentage of these campus' discretionary budget is reallocated for intervention resources, contracted services and campus professional development as decided by district leadership not campus stakeholders. On such a campus, school reform efforts rely heavily on standardized test results (Bloom & Owens, 2011). To some degree, higher order thinking skills, creative instructional practices, and shared leadership are discouraged from low achieving campuses. Staff members, including campus leadership, are relegated to curriculum managers monitoring fidelity of district adopted intervention programs. With dozens of principal reassignments and demotions made during my tenure, I witnessed leaders avoiding taking risks and forfeiting student advocacy in favor of generalized compliance.

SIGNIFICANCE OF SHARED EXPERIENCES

Minority students are not provided with an adequate number of role models and are at times segregated within their own race. Their role models may be limited to food service workers, cashiers, blue collar workers or custodians. The 2000 U.S. Census data from one of my previous assigned campuses reported that only 3.3% of the zip code's population had attained a bachelor's degree or higher and only 40.6% of the population 25 years or older had attained a high school diploma (http://www.factfinder.census. gov). Delgado-Gaitan (2001) reported that role models coming from the community are powerful examples for historically marginalized students because they exemplify success in the system and may provide a bridge between the culture and language at home to school. This does not suggest that white teachers should be left out or cannot be effective. The home-school partnership is not dependent on shared culture alone; it requires effective and consistent communication between parents and teachers based on clear expectations from each stakeholder (Delgado-Gaitan, 2001). Additionally, students may live in inadequate conditions, stressful family situations and suffer racial or ethnic repression on campus (Valenzuela, 1999).

Only a leader with shared experiences or a true advocate for social-justice would prioritize resources and efforts to negate the delivery of a pedagogy of poverty. Without leaders present to promote diversity, this watered-down curriculum is reinforced by oblivious educators threatening students' educational attainment. As a first-year principal of a struggling campus, community pride and showcasing cultural assets were of greater importance than academic outcomes. This is not to suggest that academic progress and performance were not important to our campus program. As leader, I made the decision to risk my status and career aspirations within the school district with conviction and a full belief that the result of our nontraditional approaches of academic interventions and community involvement would be improved and sustained academic achievement. Specifically, campus funds for items such as office furniture, leadership professional development and extra-duty pay for accelerated instruction were used to directly provide students with culturally based experiences such as Mariachi instruction, mural and visual art, hip-hop and flash mob dance, yoga, tamaladas, and fees for community street fairs. These events were documented as tutoring and sponsored by certified faculty members but involved community members willing to share their gifts to nurture community and self-pride in our students. Schedules and rosters were adjusted to allow for all students to experience events during school hours. We negotiated with our food service manager to allow for parents to access our facilities as food was an integral component of our events. Year after year and supervisor after supervisor I was threatened with reassignment but was willing to sacrifice my title if needed.

My resilience was rooted in my connection to the community. I was born less than a mile from the campus and had family members attending a cluster of neighboring schools including our middle school and high school feeder pattern. Without doubt, I knew that true change could only emerge from courageous leadership. In addition, I consciously strived to model this approach to leadership for faculty, staff, students, and the community.

PROFESSIONAL AND CULTURAL LEADERSHIP DUALITY

Knowledge of organization theory is essential for effective management of any organization, particularly one in need of significant improvement or transformation. It is well understood that reactionary styles of management are counterproductive to the anticipated goals of the organization. Knowledge of organization theories allows for leaders to develop plans that encompass modern ideologies in advanced technology, communication, and social influences for organizational transformation necessary in struggling campuses.

As a campus leader in the K–12 educational system, I can attest to the benefits of becoming familiar with diverse organizational theories in leadership. Inheriting campuses ranked near the bottom of a school district made up of 91 campuses provided challenging yet rewarding leadership opportunities. To an outsider, the immediate matters of concern seemed to be academic performance and the limited skill set in teaching, planning, assessment, and data analysis of the faculty. These types of deficiencies can be easily addressed with targeted professional development and timely monitoring of implementation followed by data analysis and interpretation; however, the deficiencies were outcomes of deeper organizational deficiencies.

In my professional role as a leader I referenced traditional organization theories to support the development of our plan of action. As we planned, I was also able to evaluate our projected strategies and activities through a cultural leader lens. Based on my leadership experiences on struggling campuses and reviewing the various organization theories from my leadership preparation program, the two organization theories of (1) human resource theory and (2) organizational culture and change theory emerged as frameworks ideal for addressing our campus academic achievement aligned with cultural advocacy.

Human resource theory is based on the behaviors and motivations of humans in the system or organization. Selznick (1948) argues that although classical theories could rationally design an organization, these theories could not address the nonrational components of the organization such as conflicting goals and aspirations of individuals with those of the organization. Humans and organizations needed each other for advancement and to meet each other's needs. If the worker is dissatisfied, the organization suffers and vice versa creating an interdependent relationship. Human behavior is motivated by needs which can determine the level of motivation of the worker (Maslow, 1943; McGregor, 1957). Leadership can tap into these needs by including the employee in the decision-making process allowing esteem or ego needs to be fulfilled. Developing relationships between the employee and leadership will benefit the organization in the long term by delegating responsibility and utilizing the worker as a resource beyond physical labor (Follett, 1926; McGregor, 1957). This approach became the foundation of how we developed our improvement plan, managed our budget and coordinated our professional development sessions and community events.

Our site-based leadership team developed our annual calendar of events based on data collected through after-action reviews. The site-based leadership team included members of our faculty and staff, community members, parents, and students. This team met monthly without fail and twice a month from April to June. All decisions made with respect to our campus wide events emerged from these meetings. It was also the responsibility of this team to allocate funds, as appropriate, to support these events. Professional development was also coordinated by this team based on campus data in areas such as attendance, behavior, parent, and student surveys, as well as formative and summative assessments. We also evaluated our activities and budget with our campus shared vision in mind as a means to assure stakeholders that our words were aligned with our actions. Our meeting minutes, agendas, and planning sessions were open and available to any stakeholder as a form of transparency. As a member of the site-based leadership team, my voice counted as a single member of the whole, though I had authority to override decisions.

The most innovative and creative ideas came from many different stakeholders. My role became chief negotiator requesting either support from central office or strategically masking our efforts behind traditional jargon. The greater influence our stakeholders had in the development of our campus program, the more appealing our campus became to others outside of the organization. Our overall student enrollment increased every year during my tenure as did the promotion of many aspiring leaders on the campus within the school district resulting in opportunities for us to recruit high performing faculty and staff.

In organizational culture and change theory, the ideologies of organization development were now focused on the values, beliefs, assumptions, norms, artifacts, and patterns of behavior within the organization (Shafritz et al., 2011). From my experiences, the organizations or campuses developed into a system larger than academic achievement. The system was made up of interdependent components of people in the hierarchy, where decisions were based on consensus and shared information for predictable issues (Shafritz et al., 2011). Our main obstacle was implementing campus level initiatives not completely aligned with district initiatives. In some regards, the prevailing district philosophy believed that what worked for once campus would surely work at all other campuses. We strategically found ways to empower employees and share responsibility in outcomes. This approach increased accountability at the campus level developing a system of sustained progress in areas beyond state assessments such as community networking, developing a sense of belonging and community involvement.

Providing the faculty and staff with relevant professional development and integrating social justice in our campus program was my responsibility as the campus leader. Although I was trained to reference traditional organization theories to develop an effective framework for decision making and shared leadership, I was not trained how to effectively integrate a culturally relevant program to a faculty and staff serving a campus with a 98% Hispanic, 96% economically disadvantaged population. Fortunately, I was raised in the community of the campus and was able to access shared experiences and the common language I had with the campus community. My familiarity with the community led to differences in opinion between central office leadership and me. It was from these differences that I learned that although some leaders appear similar to those they serve, they can be counterproductive to the advancement of the community. Interestingly, acculturation and assimilation among teachers is not solely reinforced by white teachers but from teachers of different racial groups as well including Hispanic teachers as they too have become acculturated and assimilated into the mainstream culture (Garcia & Guerra, 2004). Garcia and Guerra (2004) found that these educators, at times, harm children more than overt Americanization approaches as they promote "caring" for the marginalized students at the expense of high expectations resulting in low academic performance.

Cultural relevance becomes an important skill for campus leaders, faculty, and staff. Ladson-Billings(2009) shared the following key terms with the reader: (1) culturally congruent-teachers alter speech patterns or communication styles to resemble those of the students (2) cultural appropriateness-using styles for teaching similar to communication styles at students' homes (3) cultural responsiveness/cultural compatibility-making schools more accessible to culturally diverse learners (4) cultural synchronization-teachers styles and cultural awareness are in sync with students cultural needs and learning styles. Finally, the term "cultural relevance" is evident in the behaviors of those teachers not only addressing cultural differences, but also nurturing these differences and working to transcend negative effects of the dominant culture.

Ladson-Billings (2009) discussed the issue of racism critical of those who responded that they saw no color, or they treated everyone the same. This color blindness or "dysconscious racism" becomes a matter of concern in its own right. Ladson-Billings attributed the strength of culturally relevant teachers as being able to not only acknowledge differences in race but being able to provide each culture with its specific needs for access and success in the education system.

CONCLUSION

Leaders must evaluate their campus to determine which other factors are contributing to campus failure. The cultural competence of campus leaders plays a role in the development of effective plans for the teaching and learning of underserved populations. A campus leader may state their plan and intent to advocate for social justice, yet after further review find that their ethnocentric and ethno-relative orientations are not aligned with the concepts of social justice. Cultural awareness, shared experiences with those served and familiarity with the concept of professional and cultural leadership duality all contribute to the success of those tasked with the admirable opportunity to lead campuses that serve marginalized populations.

Additionally, providing professional development for staff and campus leaders on the concepts of space and marginalization will assist in the development of a campus culture sensitive to cultural diversity. Failure to acknowledge these concepts may result in intensified perceptions of student marginalization (Venzant Chambers & McCready, 2011). It is important for leaders to approach racial subgroups with lens of diversity and critically consider if any campus policies and procedures privilege particular groups leading to a sense of isolation for others (Venzant Chambers & McCready, 2011).

Though traditional leadership preparation programs and organization theories are essential in developing a framework for shared leadership and resource allocation, it is of utmost important for leaders to advocate for social justice. Not all students have access to the same resources needed to make informed decisions about their education (Perez & McDonough, 2008). Friends and family create a support system for all students as they navigate through the educational system. This creates disparity among those families with a wide network of people and community resources as compared to those with limited to no significant resources. Marginalized or underserved groups are limited in support and guidance as to what types of questions to ask and what types of aspirations the set for themselves. They lack family members or access to adults who have successfully navigated through the educational system. As stated, it is critical for campus leaders to be enlightened in the concept of social justice to provide students with access to resources and social capital. These leaders must emphasize cultural and community strengths, defy pedagogical conformity of the leadership training as needed to advocate to those they serve, build a library of shared experiences with stakeholders, and sharpen their own skills as the professional and cultural leader of the campus.

REFERENCES

Bloom, C. & Owens, E. (2011). Principals' perception of influence on factors affecting student achievement in low- and high- achieving urban high schools. *Education and Urban Society, XX*(X), 1–26.

Brown, K., Benkovitz, J., Muttillo, A. J., & Urban, T. (2010). Leading schools of excellence and equity: Documenting effective strategies in closing achievement gaps. *Teachers College Record, 113*(1), 57–96.

Delgado-Gaitan, C. (2001). *The power of community: Mobilizing for family and schooling.* Rowman & Littlefield.

Follett, M. (1926). The giving of orders. *Scientific foundations of business administration.* Williams and Wilkins.

Freire, P. (2010). *Pedagogy of the oppressed.* Continuum.

Gabbard, D. (2008). *Knowledge & power in the global economy: The effects of school reform in a neoliberal/neoconservative age.* Lawrence Erlbaum Associates.

Garcia, S. B., & Guerra, P. L. (2004). Deconstructing deficit thinking: Working with educators to create more equitable learning environments. *Education and Urban Society, 36*, 150–168.

Hernandez, F., & Kose, B. (2010). The developmental model of intercultural sensitivity: A tool for understanding principals' cultural competence. *Education and Urban Society, XX*(X), 1–19.

Howard, T. C. (2010). *Why race and culture matter in schools: Closing the achievement gap in America's classrooms.* Nw York, NY: Teachers College Press.

Ladson-Billings, G. (2009). *The dream keepers: Successful teachers of African American children.* Jossey-Bass.

Maslow, A. (1943). A theory of human motivators. *Psychological Review, 50*, 370–396.

McGregor, D. (1957). The human side of enterprise. *Management Review, 46*, 22–28.

Morgan, J. (2000). Critical pedagogy: The spaces that make the difference. *Pedagogy, Culture and Society, 8*(3), 273–289.

Perez, P., & McDonough, P. (2008). Understanding Latina and Latino college choice: A social capital and chain migration analysis. *Journal of Hispanic Higher Education, 7*(3), 249–265.

Selznick, P. (1948). Foundations of the theory of organization. *American Sociological Review 13*, 25–35.

Shafritz, J., Ott, J., & Jang, Y. (2010). *Classics of organization theory.* Wadsworth.

Spring, J. (2011). *The American school: A global context from the Puritans to the Obama era.* McGraw-Hill.

United States Census Data. (2000). http://www.factfinder.census.gov

Valenzuela, A. (1999). *Subtractive schooling: US-Mexican youth and the politics of caring.* State University of New York Press.

Venzant Chambers, T., & McCready, L. T. (2011). Making space for ourselves: African American student responses to their marginalization. *Urban Education, 46*(6), 1352–1378.

CHAPTER 10

DARE TO DREAM
AND KEEP IT MOVING

From GED to EdD

C. Dedra Williams

During the first phase of the doctoral program, I was initially ashamed to reveal that fact that I never received my high school diploma. I was forced to obtain a GED as result of my refusal to submit to cavalier instruction and various instances of bureaucracy and ineptitude during my final high school years Although I am a professed life-long learner, I used to think it was quite audacious or beyond my wildest dreams to attempt to evolve from GED to EdD, Based on my current research of critical race theory (CRT), I found that I had ingrained, preconceived notions about myself based upon the frustrating aspects of schooling (Ladson-Billings, 2005; Tate, 2005; Tatum, 1992). Moreover, during my educational journey, I was able to search myself to answer the profound questions: Who are you? How did you get here? What is your purpose in education? Where are you going?

Upon completing the benchmark, I process and entering leadership seminar, I finally felt comfortable with my position as a leader with a voice that actually mattered. The culmination of the first phase of the doctoral

Purveyors of Change: School Leaders of Color Share Narratives of Student, School, and Community Success, pp. 85–100
Copyright © 2021 by Information Age Publishing

process brought my concealed ideas about the significance of using spirituality, emotional intelligence, and patience to the forefront as active
qualities of my leadership styles. Leadership seminar helped me to realize
that diverse life experiences can contribute to the conceptual framework
of leadership. An honest and accurate awareness of myself developed into
a platform that encompasses theories of social justice, servant-leadership,
feminism, and ethics of care. The merging interconnections of these
philosophies have encouraged me to question the connections between
society and education. Education encompasses everyone and collaborative
social thought will help everyone to become actively involved promoting
positive goals for schooling (Noddings, 2003). Schools are supposed to
help students to recognize that education extends beyond the classroom
walls, home life and community; positive school goals motivate students to
expand their knowledge of self as well as their connections to the broader
society.

My first schooling experience at a predominantly African American
inner city school failed to transfer the knowledge that the person who
understands that things all over the world have an effect on one's own
block, on one's financial status, on one's acceptance or rejection into
society, has a greater chance of being a success. Perhaps, because I was
not from a well-known, well-connected, or large family in my town, the
scope of my "reality" was limited. Within the confines of social justice and
democracy, the essential questions about the education of *all* should be
"who benefits?" and "who suffers?" Perhaps a deeper connotation based
upon critical reflection and analysis of more intense questions such as,
"Who is repressed?" and "Who determines 'reality'?"

DuBois (1903) discussed this type of mindset in an excerpt from "The
Talented Tenth" by suggesting that the "most capable" of African Americans
must be schooled and prepared to attend colleges and universities. DuBois
continues that The Talented Tenth "rises and pulls all that are worth saving
up to their vantage ground" (p. 79). Some educators did not believe that
need for my dimensions in learning needed to be broadened because of
their perception of who I was and who I was going to become as evidenced
by contrived notions about my ethnicity and socioeconomic status. DuBois
stated, "human education is not simply a matter of schools; it is much more
a matter of family and group life-the training of one's home, of one's daily
companions, of one's social class" (p. 79)

It was not until I experienced a drastic change in my educational
learning environment and demographic area that I noticed I was able to
see society and myself from a different perspective. In my previous school
environment, cultural stability and predictability helped to shape my
identity. However, after being removed from my cultural realm and being
introduced to multiculturalism, I gained a deeper insight about culture,

education, and the concept of leadership. The transfer of schools introduced me to my first critical experience with reflective thinking.

Reflective thought, according to Dewey (1910), is "active, persistent and careful consideration of any belief or supposed form of knowledge in the light of the grounds that support it, and the further conclusions to which it tends, constitutes reflective thought" (p. 6). Displacement from what I perceived as a normal environment and school community was the beginning of transformation. I was challenged to become a better student, a more caring person who was cognizant of other cultures with a different image of community. Palmer (1998) uses a poem by Mary Oliver entitled "Wild Geese" in *The Courage to Teach*. The first two lines of the poem, "Whoever you are, no matter how lonely, the world offers itself to your imagination" (p. 89) best describes my feelings during my transformation process. Once the reflective thought process started, I was able to establish my belief system consciously about caring, serving, and appreciating others in my personal and professional life "upon the firm basis of reason" (Dewey, 1910).

As a former "at-risk" student, lifelong learner, and current educator, I see a need for resourceful techniques to meet the demands of diversification in educational paradigm shifts. "At risk" students usually earn this title because they stem from so-called grim socioeconomic conditions. I learned that I was an "at-risk" student when I was promoted to the middle school. My grandmother was my primary caretaker while my single mother worked 53 hours a week. My guidance counselor informed me that since I was reared in a female dominated home without a "father figure," I was destined to have academic and social maladjustments that would place me in the "at-risk" category. The term "at-risk" was defined as one who was "at-risk" of future failures.

The transformation of my thinking occurred when I was able to realize that I was subjected to certain life conditions that may have been oppressive if I did not equate the value of education with success. Connecting education with success as well as stability helped me to develop as a leader because I could never accept being thwarted by static mindsets about educators and the educated. Interconnectedness is essential to effective leadership because relationships between leaders and followers are enhanced as both groups are able to grow by developing valuable judgments, improved confidence and most importantly, trust (Giuliani, 2002; Lencioni, 2002; Stowell & Mead, 2007).

Building a sense of acceptance, community, respect, and value of differences does not seem to be at the academic forefront within all levels of schooling and aspects of society. In some cases, embarrassing situations, problems, or affronts must occur before most can recall the purpose and meaning of "social justice for all." If educational leaders considered the impact that we have on the lives of all that we encounter, we may become more aware of our actions, deeds, and treatment (or mistreatment) of people. An analysis of the leadership styles of Lincoln and Giuliani provided insight about evolving as a leader due to circumstances. Although both Lincoln and Giuliani were often subjected to scrutiny and criticism, they both managed to discover who they were and why they chose to make decisions in the manner in which they chose with sound reason. They both exhibited exceptional self-awareness and emotional intelligence, which was crucial to their monumental success both as leaders and as individuals who impacted the world.

The profound actions and noteworthy leadership styles of Abraham Lincoln as well as Guiliani (2002) remind leaders that they must have a willingness to accept and uphold responsibility. Leaders as well as followers have a responsibility to each other (Giuliani, 2002; Lencioni, 2002; Stowell & Mead, 2007). Giuliani's (2002) six principles of leadership: strong beliefs, optimism, bravery and courage, relentless preparation, teamwork, and communication are basic tenets that enable me to continue teaching students and motivating educators. Moreover, Burns (1978) notes when persons are engaged with others in an exchange as leaders and followers, the relationship raises one another to higher levels of motivation and moral principles which help to address and fulfill human need. According to Useem (1998), connectedness is a part of that fulfillment because it reflects "who we are and what we do" and "is related to our effectiveness" (p. 231) as leaders with a vision. Connectedness also helps leaders and followers recognize that there is a power greater than ourselves, and we may have to go through changes in life to understand our purpose (Begley, 2005; Giuliani, 2002; Jaworski, 1996; Jentz, 2006; Palmer,1998; Useem,1998; Whitfield, 2003),

When I was removed from my natural comfortable environment, my concept of power, purpose and trust became strained. My first thought was of betrayal because I was forced to be uncomfortable in a new learning environment that positioned me to deal with different learning expectations, behavioral changes and diverse cultures; however, I had to relearn how to develop trust. The learning process occurred when I was able to share and gain information about others and me. Moreover, I realized that I had to develop trust in order to have meaningful relationships that would enable me to survive. Trust, I have learned, has to transcend ethnic, cultural, gender, and age differences because it is one of the most powerful aspects of any relationship, especially in terms of leadership connections. Robert Greenleaf (1977) suggested that people tend to " 'freely respond' to individuals in the leadership role because they have been "proven and trusted as servants" (p. 20).

I believe that if individuals who are grounded in faith and facilitate necessary changes, they will attempt to ensure that education is equitable for all capable learners. In a metaphorical sense, the face of education, once bright and strong, is showing change. It is growing old. It is exhibiting signs of being weak, weary, and tired; it is time for a facelift. Education can be viewed as a birth to death experience for everyone. Although living and learning are constantly changing, it is important to realize that these two components of existence must continuously coincide. Analyzing ourselves including our relationships to others through critical theory "requires us to reflect on what we do and how what we do affects all who encounters us" (Foster, 1986, p. 70). Although the application of situational leadership has enabled me to use what my colleagues termed "differentiated supervision" for positive outcomes, struggles still surfaced as I contended with the complexities of change.

In a leadership role, it is difficult to find a sense of balance concerning care with power; however, the combinations of both are the most essential components of effective leadership. "Caring power" is a term that I first discovered in the work of Sernak (1998) who notes, "Caring connoted relation, connectedness, concern, giving and receiving" and power is often associated with "authority, control, domination, force, and ultimately, oppression" (p. 127). The term "caring power" resulted as part of the conundrum about the relationship of caring and power. As a new school administrator, I found that the concept of caring power has aided in my shift from the teacher, an individual acting on my own, to the servant leader, a person concerned about the good of the collective. In a short time, I have developed relationships that include the reciprocation of nurturing and support because I would like for individuals to appreciate the sense of being a part of a "caring community."

By encouraging professional growth and harmonious relationships, I have "reconceptualized" what others thought was leadership based upon traditional standards. I have come to realize, although I am in a position of "authority," that I must exercise the combination of caring and power to change the climate within my school (Sernak, 1998). Additionally, the study of the "power with" concept has enhanced my understanding of treatment of power and leadership because it "challenges us to reexamine our understanding of power as it relates to culture, domination, hegemony, ideology, resistance and liberation" (Kreisberg, 1992, p. 87).

I know that I have power and the ability to care, but as a leader I must recognize that my role can change at any given time. At times, I may have to be leader while in others it may behoove me to be a follower. "Leadership is based on a shared culture and does not result from position or power" (Foster, 1986, p. 182). I have to care and appreciate the idea of individual and group actions and be mindful that I must respect the areas of expertise that others have to offer and the "life-worlds" that contributed to their mindsets about schooling.

The overall concept of caring has provided insight about my colleagues who exist with or have overcome a variety of life experiences. Grogan (2000) found that many during the course of their lives may have contended with marginalization experiences that include "poverty, disability, ethnicity, gender, and sexual orientation" (p. 133). Grogan suggested that you should not treat people with various conditions in a "universal manner." This mindset has enabled me to use my role to promote the idea that we are individuals who are a part of collective and who care about improving opportunities for all in education. An ethic of care has been established within the departments that I supervise because I deal with colleagues as if they are individuals who are a part of a relationship that is independent of their respective department or as Grogan would suggest "not as representatives of social groups" (p. 133).

However, I believe that I relate to theories about caring and the ethics of care because of my gender and the composition of my social constructs. African American women are known to be dominant forces within their culture primarily because during the period of enslavement women often had to function without men; they were considered the head of household. They had to be caring to their children and to others who relied upon their care while maintaining the power and will to survive. Spirituality and religion provided sources of powerful direction for African American women from historical to contemporary times (Capper et al., 2002; Sernak, 1998).

Eugene (1989) as cited in Sernak (1998) contended that the relationship of African American women to religion is "one involving endurance, resistance, and resiliency in the face of personal and institutional domination." Sernak notes that the "recognition of the impact of cultural differences is essential to the understanding of caring, power, and their intersection" (p. 144). "Caring power" takes into account personal, spiritual, and religious motives and encourages fairness for all members of society; it encourages me to be a truth seeker.

An excerpt from my career exemplifies my connections related to caring, power, culture, faith, and leadership development as follows:

> Faith, instilled by my grandmother, from my inception through the continuum of my life enabled me to have confidence and courage in any given situation. My grandmother imbedded in my brain the scripture, "I can do all things through Christ who strengthens me" (Philippians 4:13) and "Let us not love with words or tongue but with actions and in truth." (1 John 4:6)

However, during life's journey, I would often forget my faith because I thought that I had relinquished myself to the oppression of power, cultural entrenchment, and subjectivism. Societal ills and pressures, stature and stereotypes were supposed to consume and define me. However, my academic and social experiences with heterogeneous peers and the critical evaluation of education from all vantage points in my life has led to transformation and continuation of my desire to be an observer, learner, educator, and ultimately a strong, sincere leader. Past and present experiences are simultaneously directing my future aspirations to use my knowledge of sociocultural aspects to improve personal and professional relationships. The disposition of open-mindedness helps to ensure that I, as well as others, are prepared the meet plurality of educational expectations and societal demands because I believe that there is more than one kind of reality in terms of the values that society places on equitable education all people.

My beliefs have encouraged me to make choices that do not feed egos or seek acceptance but to critical opposition, opinions, uplift others, and contribute to the greater collective. I am truly satisfied make a difference, develop others, and contribute to a positive vision. My motivation to serve others and create shared goals within my school is evidenced by the impact of "servant-leadership," a term coined by Greenleaf (1977) and its effects on my personal and professional life.

Greenleaf's (1977) theories about servant leadership such as leading by serving others, accomplishing goals by serving others, and encouraging others to use their talents to accomplish common goals while recognizing the needs of others and fostering their growth as outstanding individuals have become a part of my leadership style. However, after some research and reflection, I realized that I had been introduced to the concept of "servant-leadership" prior to taking my first doctoral class. Prior to preschool, my grandmother introduced me to my first life application of "servant-leadership" by introducing me to the Bible and Psalm 23 (NAB), which reads:

> The LORD is my shepherd; there is nothing I lack. In green pastures you let me graze; to safe waters you lead me; you restore my strength. You guide me along the right path for the sake of your name. Even when I walk through a dark valley, I fear no harm for you are at my side; your rod and staff give me courage. You set a table before me as my enemies watch; You anoint my head with oil; my cup overflows. Only goodness and love will pursue me all the days of my life; I will dwell in the house of the LORD for years to come.

The ethics of care are evidenced by the figurehead of the shepherd who cares for his assigned flock. The shepherd has a concern about people and the ability to facilitate changes and movement. The shepherd is also one who God has entrusted to be committed and responsible for others. The "right path" mentioned in the Scripture has the connotative meaning of doing things the right way or the most ethical way. The "dark valley" could mean that when you choose "the right way" in a leadership capacity, it is a difficult path to follow because it some cases it can become lonely and dreadful. The setting of the table motif could relate to meeting that leaders must attend to conduct business. "You set a table before me as my enemies watch" could connote that while people may meet and try to build relationships and communities to promote positive goals for the greater good, enemies such as bureaucracy, social, personal, and political agendas, racism, classism, sexism, ageism, and the like continue to loom within various organizational cultures. The oil and the overflowing cup could encourage one to believe that he will be ultimately rewarded for having courage in the face of adversity. As result, "goodness" and "love" become a part of the decision-making process when the concerns of others are being addressed which gives consideration for the need for the ethics of care, social justice, and servant-leadership.

My grandmother encouraged me to implement the principles of Psalm 23 into my philosophy about character, confidence, and the treatment of others. My reflections of this Scripture combined with the work of Greenleaf (1977) prompted an evaluation myself as a professional in education who has been placed in a leadership position. I have come to the realization that to have an opportunity to lead could be a blessing because effective leadership can inspire, negotiate, and bring about positive changes within various organizations.

Bennis (1989) suggests that "vision, inspiration, empathy and trustworthiness" are characteristics of effective leadership practices (p. 140). I liken myself to the shepherd in Psalm 23 because I think beyond the day-to-day realities of school life and I have disciplined myself to maintain focus and clarity of perceptions in regards to schooling. If I become engrossed in the mundane, I realize that my abilities to dream of a positive, productive school community may be destroyed. History, politics, and social issues can impose their views on schools; therefore, devaluing the importance of schools as the major contributor of developing potential and human lives.

Building a community with people within my school is crucial to the success of the students as well as the overall school population. Prior to becoming an administrator, I recognized that people did not want to interact with each other based upon interpersonal and intrapersonal differences. However, during the course of my career, I knew that I had to be prepared to accept the call and dare to communicate to others (especially the most resistance ones). I often remind my colleagues that we, as community and collective, have the power to keep the promise to work together to create a more caring school environment that is conducive to the needs of all.

Greenleaf (1977) stated, "All that is needed to rebuild community as a viable life form for large numbers of people is for enough servant leaders to show the way, not by mass movements, but by each servant-leader demonstrating his or her unlimited liability for a quite specific community related group" (p. 77). Sernak (1998) suggested that caring leaders think beyond their personal gain to establish a community that is "collaborative rather than competitive." Care encourages leaders to connect self to community members to become "joint guardians" of their school and society because they realize that both aspects of life are essential branches of the world (Kreisberg, 1992). Palmer (1998) suggested that spirituality allows for a community to embrace and value differences or a "communities of truth" that are comprised of "diversity, ambiguity, creative conflict, honesty, humility and freedom" (p. 107).

The connections between my sense of spirituality and my experiences within my community from my formative years have a major influence on my leadership style. Capper et al. (2002) supports my assumption in noting that "spirituality and community offers us the space from which we can challenge our assumptions and our thinking about, reconsider our practices for, and plan action for a more excellent and equitable place we call 'school'" (p. 92). Spiritually, service, and work have been the combined philosophical basis of my varied commitments of caring about people. Greenleaf (1977) reminds me that I, as a leader, am no greater than the people that I serve. I care about the intrinsic value of people because my life experiences have taught me that many can make tangible contributions to life and school experiences.

My concepts about the use of care link social justice to my leadership platform because I have experienced inequities in education. As a result of my school experiences and my faith, I was able to develop an ethic to hope and succeed. I often reflect on my educational experiences from various perspectives such as physical presence, race, class, locality, ethnicity, language, and culture. I have even given consideration about my last name beginning with a "W" which meant that I was always the last to be called and usually was placed at the end of the line. Given my diminutive stature, I often wondered if the repetition of such treatment might have had any impact on my esteem or social and academic growth during my formative years.

Pondering about these past concerns have contributed to my present critical awareness and concern about how children are being treated in every aspect of schooling. Grogan (2000) best summarizes the action that I must take because of commitment to social justice because I have "to ask tough questions, to consider multiple perspectives, and to put [myself] on the line" (p. 133). Taking a stand for social justice has encouraged me to ask questions of students, parents, colleagues, and administrators to communicate the need for change of past, traditional, ineffective practices.

Social justice has also become one of the guiding forces in my life. Social justice stimulated my desire to embark upon ethnographic travel to different places in the world to gain a deeper insight about the treatment of people and the relationship between education and society from the global perspective. My understanding of the global perspectives helps me to dispel some of the stereotypical myths that some educators have about children who are culturally, ethnically, or linguistically diverse. My interaction with the world has changed my perception of self and others (Dewey, 1914, 1916/1944). With the mass influx of culturally and linguistically diverse students into the mainstream population, leaders must take into consideration "how differing voices contribute to a better understanding of pluralistic contexts" (Grogan, 2000 p. 133).

Most culturally and linguistically diverse students within my school are often slighted because the current organizational structures have created cultural norms and expectations that are inequitable and oppressive in nature. Some believe that certain students are not worthy of challenging; not capable of passing standardized tests; nor worthy of respect, dignity, and the efforts of providing quality instruction. When I am faced with adversity about ensuring equity in education, I put learning and theory into practice. I often revisit the qualities of servant leadership as found in the shepherd archetype and contemplate the correct use of power for the situation.

My theories about the implementation of power and servant leadership are exemplified in the qualities of the shepherd. Although shepherding has the authority and control to direct or redirect the flock, the shepherd must recognize that he has work in conjunction with the masses in order to reach the goal of group which is safe passage to a new territory. As a caring leader, I find that having a sense of trust, genuine caring, confidence, motivation, and valuing people, being tough, assertive, accountable, and focused helps me to build relationships. Recognizing the emotional impact of placing demands on others has helped to determine how much power and influence I have to use to implement changes and reach goals. Power becomes meaningful when it evolves from the followers. Power becomes meaningful when it evolves from the followers. For example, the shepherd knows how to use his power based upon the temperament of the flock.

Being an innovator and enthusiast is one of my most daunting task because I engage and challenge people by presenting new ideas about instructional delivery, discussing current research, encouraging others to pursue their dreams and cultivate their talents, and asking for their valuable input about enriching lives by sharing, teaching and learning.

Sometimes, I find that my theories about caring and servant leadership are foreign to those with whom I most interact because it is often met with respectable resistance.

Some authoritative figures in schools do not have the patience or concern to be bothered with taking time to think and care before possible making a life altering decision. Although all educators acknowledge that change is constant, few people have mapped out its impact. Some of my colleagues do not understand the pressing dilemmas such as achieving local, state, and federal standards and providing unification of extreme diversity, supporting the roles of teachers and facilitating the changing teachers' roles. Some narrow-minded people believe that providing free lunch and bus tickets to students with a low socioeconomic status covers social justice. I am enthusiastic about ensuring that all students are exposed to a learning environment that is rich and conducive to their needs. However, my enthusiasm is not shared; the plight of underserved populations is rarely considered unless there is a problem that needs to be addressed before negligence and apathy are exposed.

Most people are reluctant to share enthusiasm or passion about gaining new insights about people from diverse cultures and populations and ensuring equity of underserved populations. My background, experience and social knowledge enable me to provide insight about "others" within the school. I am aware that if I, as an African American female, was not on the administrative team some political, cultural, and social issues would not be brought to the forefront. I recognize the pluralistic significance of my voice, obligation to care, and "positional power." Leaders with insight and awareness can use their positional power to encourage others to gain knowledge and experience of persons from other cultures and backgrounds. As a servant leader, I do not use positional power often because I rely more on persuasion. I like to build a consensus within groups and convince others that we have a shared purpose within the school, and we all have significant roles that help to fulfill various purposes of teaching, learning, sharing, and growing.

My servant leadership requires me to take action to "stretch [myself] and [my] people." Although [servant leaders] never expect more from a person than that person is capable of performing, they often expect more than that person believes that he or she can accomplish. This is [the servant leaders] key for developing the confidence and ability in individuals and helping them to obtain a maximum "feeling of accomplishment" (Batten, 1996, p. 39). Some individuals are not receptive about my desire to truly understand people and consider their value. Batten (1996) noted,

> Servant-leaders continually strive to attain a better understanding of peo-
> ple and their differences-to determine what it takes to impel each person to

produce and create. They recognize that many people need to be stretched, helped, encouraged, and sometimes pressured to reach out and grasp the opportunities all around them. (p. 40)

Servant leadership is not a part of my school culture and I am often questioned about my motives and treatment of people because I am not behaving in the traditional manner. However, some administrators have stopped avoiding the need for a dialogue about individual and group differences because when given a chance I make mention that we cannot grow personally, professionally or as a society if we do not attempt to take action to make improvements within our school and society. Although I am constantly challenged by other teachers and administrators about actually serving as a leader, I refuse to compromise my position of being concerned about the development of students' social, emotional, physical, moral, and academic capabilities and limiting achievement disparities.

Another challenge to my combined theories is related to my use of the ethics of care. The culture of my school, in terms of administration, is predominantly driven by males. My choice to be a caring female is a difficult task because conceivably my natural gender responsiveness may prompt me to have a need to affirm, protect, and provide compassion that some males may challenge because they deem my actions as unnecessary. Sernak (1998) suggested that "caring as collective effort is difficult, for it becomes a *politics* of caring, disturbing traditional male-female relationships and, more important, challenging the presumed 'femaleness' of caring."

I believe that some situations require sensitivity and emotional responsiveness because these aspects of care can serve as a guide to actions that are morally acceptable. I find that caring makes me alert to circumstances because it removes the detached attitude that may be traditionally associated with being an administrator. I can resolve conflicts and disputes more effectively when care encourages me to seek alternative, ethical approaches to mediate problems.

However, in a male hierarchy, care may not be driving force in their decision-making processes. In some cases, a gender power struggle seems to ensue when sensitive issues arise during formal meetings and informal dialogues. In Sernak's (1998) discussion about gender-neutral as aspects of caring-power notes that "women, primarily, discuss school reform in terms of caring, while a preponderance of men speaks in terms of power, albeit in the form of empowerment" (p. 169). Care requires time, thought, and effort; some male administrators seem to be a bit frustrated when I do not provide an immediate response to a given situation. Often, I have to rationalize with my male counterparts about the need to understand the value of demonstrating care and to become more cognizant about the use of care.

I have to spend unnecessary time and energy about trying find meaning in conversations. I feel like I am using energy and power and not moving toward my goals and dreams. I am not an idealist dreamer; however, I am adamant about my dreams of being an effective leader who is a part of progressive schooling. I have to strive to find the realistic balance between my desires that practical and those that are challenging. I synergize my emotions and sense of balance through prayer, conversations, recalling experiences, and energizing myself by deferring to my interests and imaginings (Jaworski, 1996; Jentz, 2006). Nothing much can to fruition without a dream. If something monumental is going to happen in terms of change, you have to be bold enough to dream and believe (Greenleaf, 1977)

Daring to dream has changed the entire spectrum of all aspects of my life from my formative years to future expectations. My values and appreciation of caring, culture, learning, sharing, and growing helped to define my dream of being a successful concerned citizen despite the bleak life expectations that society as well as some educational institutions tried to beset as my destiny. My beliefs about myself actually shaped my reality. I exceeded my own vision and expectancy because I dared to hope, struggle, and keep my dreams. As educational leaders, Batten (1998) noted,

> We all need dreams, transcendent hopes, and expectations that subliminally flavor, season, and nourish all that we say and do. If that dream is made of happy expectations, it comes back to us like a boomerang. To be able to move from one point on life's continuum to next in a fairly organized and purposeful way is important to vibrant, productive living. (p. 43)

I believe that I have a purpose with passion about the interconnectedness of education and the ideals of social answerability, political agendas, racial harmony, diversity, equitable education, and unselfish service. Although I have encountered several disappointments, setbacks, and other life disruptions during my crossing into leadership, I still managed to maintain my passion, purpose and direction about being an educator. My childhood game of playing school and my imaginings about the various roles within a school actually transpired in a meaningful career path. My desire to be educated and successful helped me to develop and maintain a positive outlook about my life and the lives of others.

My educational philosophy and mantra is *positive education always causes elevation*. Even though it may have taken years to realize a dream of pursuing my EdD, however, the dreaming itself has been an elevating experience. Batten (1998) notes that "it is important to let ourselves dream freely and soaringly or we will not know how to use our mental, physical, and spiritual muscles with any degree of purpose, discipline, and systems" (p. 42). My dreams and the courage to pursue my imaginings have enabled me to exceed my personal, academic, social, geographical, and professional expectations. Life experiences, caring and learning has transitioned me from being the ultimate dreamer to the dream keeper.

The roles of educational leader and dream keeper are tantamount; the concepts of my forward-thinking dreams of reciprocity, respect, social justice and equity, and quality education have placed me in the forefront of my family, school, and community. My sense of imagination has increased my ability to view aspects of leadership from multiple vantages. This is crucial because it allows me to look at situations and problems from a broader perspective, and this advances my ability to become an effective, visionary leader (Bolman & Deal, 2003). I have a responsibility to motivate and collaborate with others to shape, share, and maintain sound educational visions that promote, encourage, and inspire awareness, acceptance and appreciation of self, individuals, and the broader society. As an evolving leader, I recognize and value the importance of meeting the needs of the people that I serve. Being concerned and responsive people's needs provides them with the autonomy and responsibility to realize and accomplish goals.

My spiritual and leadership mindsets are intertwined because I found that I have the same propensities of the shepherd to protect, serve, and lead because these qualities are inherent in my gender, character and culture (Sernak 1998; Useem, 1998; Wheatley, 1999; Whitfield, 2003). The spiritual metaphor of shepherding extends through my analysis of myself as a caring person and leader (Jaworski, 1996; Jentz, 2006). My effectiveness as a servant-leader is contingent upon my realization that a flock is not there to be of service to the shepherd; the shepherd is there to be of service to the flock. The concept of and virtues associated with the ethics of care, feminist theory, social justice, and servant leadership are universal, timeless, and relevant. Life applications and leadership models have provided a vision coupled with zeal that is driven by my conviction that education can transform dreams into actuality.

REFERENCES

Batten, J. (1998). Servant-leadership: A passion to serve. In L. C. Spears (Ed.), *Insights on leadership: Service, stewardship, spirit, and servant-leadership* (pp. 38–53). Wiley.

Begley, P. T. (2005). Self-knowledge, capacity and sensitivity: Prerequisites to authentic leadership by school principals. *Journal of Educational Administration, 44*(6), 570–589

Bennis, W. (1989). *On becoming a leader.* Addison-Wesley.

Bolman, L., & Deal, T. (2003). *Reframing organizations: Artistry, choice, and leadership* (3rd ed.). Jossey-Bass.

Burns, J. M. (1978). *Leadership.* Harper and Row.

Capper, C. A., Hafner, M. M., & Keyes, M. W. (2002). The role of community in spiritually centered leadership for justice. In G. Furman (Ed.), *School as community: From promise to practice* (pp. 77–94).State University of New York Press.

Dewey, J. (1910). *How we think*. D.C. Heath.

Dewey, J. (1944). Thinking in education. From *Democracy and education: An Introduction* to the philosophy of education (pp. 152–163). The Free Press. (Original work published 1916)

DuBois, W. (1903). *The talented tenth*. James Port and Company.

Foster, W. (1986). *Paradigms and promises: New approaches to educational administration*. Prometheus Books.

Giuliani, R. W. (2002). *Leadership*. Hyperion.

Greenleaf, R. (1977). Servant leadership. In T. J. Wren (Ed.), *The leader's companion: Insights on leadership through the ages* (pp. 185–188). The Free Press.

Greenleaf, R. (1977). *Servant leadership: A journey into the nature of legitimate power and greatness*. Paulist Press.

Grogan, M. (2000). Laying the groundwork for a re conception of the superintendency from feminist postmodern perspectives. *Educational Administration Quarterly 36*(1), 117–142.

Hughes, L. (1939). *The dream keeper*. Harper and Row.

Jaworski, J. (1996). *Synchronicity: The inner path of leadership*. Berrett-Koehler.

Jentz, B. (2006). Making our own minds the object of our learning: Three reasons to seek self-knowledge. In P. Kelleher & R. Van Der Bogert (Eds.), *Voices for democracy: Struggles and celebrations of transformational leaders* (pp. 230–238). Blackwell.

Ladson-Billings, G. (2005). The evolving role of critical race theory in educational scholarship. *Race Ethnicity and Education, 8*(1), 115–119.

Lencioni, P. (2002). *The five dysfunctions of a team: A leadership fable*. Jossey-Bass.

Kreisberg, S. (1992). *Power with: Toward an alternative conception of power.* In *Transforming power: Domination, empowerment and education* (pp. 55–88). State University of New York Press.

Noddings, N. (2003). *Happiness and education*. Cambridge University Press.

Palmer, P. (1998). *The courage to teach: Exploring the inner landscape of a teacher's life*. Jossey-Bass.

Sernak, K. (1998). *School leadership: Balancing power with caring*. Teachers College Press.

Stowell, S. J., & Mead, S. S. (2007). *The team approach: With team work anything is possible*. CMOE.

Tate, W. F. (2005). Ethics, engineering and the challenge of racial reform in education. *Race Ethnicity and Education, 8*(1), 121–127.

Tatum, B. D. (1992). Talking about race, learning about racism: The application of racial identity development theory in the classroom. *Harvard Educational Review, 62*(1), 1–24.

Useem, M. (1998). Nancy Barry builds women's world banking. In M. Useem (Ed.), *The leadership moment: Nine true stories of triumph and disaster and their lessons for all of us* (pp. 208–233). Times Books/Random House.

Wheatley, M. J. (1999). *Leadership and the new science: Discovering order in a chaotic world*. Berrett-Koehler.

Whitfield, P. (2003). The day the foreign devil came to class: My teaching body in China. In D. P. Freedman & M. S. Holmes (Eds.), *The teacher's body: Embodiment, authority,and identity in the academy*. (pp. 99–104) State University of New York.

CHAPTER 11

LEADING AND SURVIVING

Navigating and Surviving the Political Currents in Urban Education

Cynthia Alexander Mitchell

PORCH PLAY

As a child we all played school. There was the always teacher, the students, and the principal. However, when we played school, the five steps on the front porch was the classroom. As it would usually happen, I was the teacher who occasionally served as the principal as well. During this time, the biggest challenge was the child on the step that talked too much or did answer the questions correctly. When this happened, my role as teacher would have to shift to the role of principal. The student would always have to reflect on their behavior, apologize and then go back to their seat on the step. When I look back on those days, I realize how simple school looked from the eyes of a child. There was not a required curriculum, no standardized test and no need for the parents to intervene. If only public education was that simple.

Purveyors of Change: School Leaders of Color Share Narratives of Student, School, and Community Success, pp. 101–107
Copyright © 2021 by Information Age Publishing

My reality of schools first changed when I transferred from a middle class urban predominantly African American school in an urban city to a suburban school in Mississippi that was 99% White. This was a challenging transition for a fifth grader. For the first time in my life, I was listed as other. I can remember the exact day when I felt the blatant, well-defined separation of children in school by race. I call it the first day of school in Mississippi.

Early on I was able to distinguish the differences between the culturally infused expectations of success from the urban schools that I had previously attended, verse the forced mode of survival in the school absent of diversity in Mississippi. Did I mention that I still lived in the city, but crossed the state line every morning with my mother who was one of five African American teachers hired at my new suburban school?

During my mother's generation of educators, 20 years post *Brown vs. Board of Education*, the hardships of education were present in both the education system in my neighborhood as well as the one that I commuted to daily during my K–12 experience. The inequities in school fiscal and human resources supports, racism, and unspoken low expectations for the minority students in my dominantly white school caused my mother to make a stern proclamation to me as a child. Out of her frustration one evening she turned to me and said, "You can be anything except become teacher!" As her struggles became more evidence to her, she would animatedly remind me to go in a different direction with my life. Little did I know, the next seven years in this same system proved to be a training ground for me that would truly serve as a benefit for future survival of things to come in my career.

DEFINING REALTY

Despite the warning of my mother, I yielded to the inward calling to not just become a teacher, but a principal. While temporarily dismissing the struggles and warning, I was overjoyed at receiving the keys to my very own school. This was one of the best moments in my life. The thrill that I initially experienced felt that it was the redemption that I sought to finally verify that I had in fact made the right decision not just to teach, but also to become a principal.

Unlike the principal that I played on the porch, my excitement soon turned into a period of emotional exhaustion. The fact that I was pulled from my previous assignment six weeks before the end of the school year should have been an indication that there was a problem. Still excited. I dismissed the timing of my transition. The school that I inherited had one of the lowest rates of proficiency in not just the city, but also the state! The teachers arrived at school under the previous administration up to an hour after school began. The building was out of control and dangerous, and maintenance was not allowed in the building to fix anything.

GAINING TRACTION

One of the first things that I conceded was that I had so much to do that I needed to prioritize a manageable starting point. I learned early on as a leader that the students, directly or indirectly, have to be the nonnegotiable center of all decisions for the school. With an "F" for achievement and an "F" for a facilities grade, the logical first step was to outline those things that were working for the children and those that were not. I learned in this situation that there are only two lessons. We either do it right the first time or learn from our mistakes. Either way, even in a situation with so many challenges, there are at least small wins.

With this stance came hard lined nonnegotiable. The building had to be an optimal place for students to learn. The teachers had to publicly commit to the success of the school. Finally, the parents and the community had to participate in the solution instead of amplifying past problems in order for the school to move forward. These directions cause the need for very strategic planning, curricular adjustments, and realignment of resources and most importantly a mindset shift around the definition of success for our students. Ultimately, there was a role or assignment for everyone.

As we sat in a circle around the library in one of our initial faculty meetings, I began to share. With the desire to see the students succeed, I remember defining with my perception of seasons. I shared that I feel like both we live in and operate in seasons. I also shared that there is definitely a season to grow, build, and a season to make changes. My concluding statement was that we cannot anyway be offended by our neighbor's current season, but we have to be honest about where we are on the journey.

I wish that I could say that I got 100% buy in and that every plan worked immediately, but the reality was that my school had gained the reputation that is was the place for teachers to retire without quitting and status quo was a coveted accomplishment. By the end of the first year, with that being said, several teachers respectfully told me that their season had changed. Others retired while a few others simply quit or transferred.

For a brief moment I was challenged and wondered what to do next. So, I deferred to the wisdom of my mentor who was a retired principal who by all accounts was seen as successful. To hear her voice at that moment was as soothing as ointment on a fresh scar. I remember her advice, "People will come and go, but you never lose anything or anybody that you are supposed to keep." Mrs. Catherine Mitchell's words gave life to a seemingly dead place.

After I shared the words of wisdom with my leadership team we rededicated to the cause of success and we pushed through with a renewed sense of purpose. Hard decisions were made, and major changes included ascetic clean up and painting, ongoing professional development for teachers and outlying new systems for learning were put in place for the students. These changes did not go unnoticed. By year three and beyond, we received an award for our inclusive practices, academic achievement and we moved from the bottom five percent in the state to the top five percent for student growth. These accomplishments lead to our school being recognized by both the State Department of Education and New Leaders for New Schools. We went from being the headline story on the news, which focused on violence and poor performance to our leadership story being captured by the National Institute for School Improvement (NUISI) in a publication for Urban School Leaders.

These efforts were credited as a demonstration of how schools and classrooms can move from a deficit model to an asset-based paradigm. This created a school specific model that works for all learners in our urban setting. The space was also allowed for implementation and reform that was more congruent with the strengths that we possessed as a school and needs of the urban community in its specific context.

While the celebration of the work from the past year's accomplishments were still fresh, my greatest challenge as a leader occurred. The perfect storm was brewing before our very eyes. From a financial perspective, in the eyes of some, funding the extreme needs of a high poverty, urban school system seemed to be a seemingly unbearable burden for the city alone. This burden of a few, very concerned school board called for a plan to balance the have and the have-nots.

At a spring school board meeting there was an unexpected vote that was put on the table as a motion. Within minutes, our current school board had voted to resolve the board and relinquish its charter for our district by one vote. With no other options and by one vote, the country district was forced to assume responsibility for the city schools. As the vote passed I sat there in utter disbelief. Within months what I had known as my district for now 17 years was vanishing before my eyes.

For the next 18 months, we would feel the tension as principals around balancing academic expectations while trying to stabilize our staffs within our schools. This was an exhausting period of not knowing what was next. To make matters worse, I was the exiting President of the principals' association during first 12 of the 18 months that outlined the merger. For the next year, my role was to not only to balance the tension of my staff, but that of my colleagues as well.

The lingering questions yet remained unanswered. One of the things that I realized immediately after the announcement was made of the relinquished charter, was that we had lost our identity. Who are we? and Who will we become? The answer was simple. We did not know. We no longer had a name, and our existence had an expiration date. The challenge as a principal was to make sure the teachers understood that children still had to be educated. Since there was such an obvious void, just stabilizing the staff and parents around understand what was happening was a daily task. I remember telling everyone that our school will always have its name, our students will have a classroom and we need our teachers. While also convincing myself, there had to be a daily reminder that ultimately, we still had to continue with school even in the ambiguity of needing a name for ourselves.

The unspoken truth was that talks of school merger began in years before it actually happened. At that time, questions were swirling in the area about the division of funding which led to charges of "unequal access" to education for the city's poor and mostly minority students.

In the case of public urban education, the merger served as an instrument. This instrument has had a defined effect on the entire community. The instrument in this case was the merger of the county school district and the city school district. While the plan seemed was well intended initially. The implication could literally either build this community or destroy it. Today, years after the merger, it is hard to identify who won because there are so many people that are affected by the effects of the action.

CATHEDRAL DAMAGE

The merger which only lasted 12 month before the ultimate demerger had the potential to provide us the opportunity to identify inefficiencies in the organizational practices, to correct fiscal policies, and develop solutions to address the economic/racial divide in the county. Instead the merger, like a magnifying glass forcing the radiant heat from the sun to converge on one spot, creating havoc. The merger created a new power dynamic as the two-system struggled in what could be compared to an arranged marriage that would ultimately lead to a divorce. The anxious climate created tug of war with the goal of winning control of the new system. In this method of leadership, the person that was chosen to lead, be it legacy county schools or city schools would also dictate the direction of the entire department. The undercurrent was whoever led an arm brought with them historical background. So, their historical base became the dominant force in the environment. Consequently, the merger also shifted the focus from educating students to adult survival.

In my new role, I had to be intentional about validating the past without jeopardizing the future. Each of my 19 principals that I supervised were from a totally different side of the merger. In some cases, I feel like this was one of the most difficult assignments issued. I prayed daily for grace to sustain me. Once again, I had gone from that majority to the other. It was during these times that I reverted back to the lessons that I learned as a fifth grader that help me to navigate the adult culture without feeling like I had reverted back to the category of other again.

REDEMPTION'S SONG

I respected the fact that each player in that merger narrative entered with a different perspective and a different fear. Where my new team saw the merger as a hostile takeover, my colleagues on the city side, felt like they had surrendered. Each experience was legitimate, but the balance came in developing a mutual respect for both sides. The role as the leadership director created the space for my team to admit that "nobody ever asked us what we thought, no one ever asked us what we wanted, and they just assumed that it was best for them is best."

With these candid conversations, we were able to draw the conclusion that this challenge affected everyone, most importantly the students. The merger shined a light on all the students. Students were no longer just kids from the city students or county students. It was no longer Black students and White students. The conversation moved towards equity for all students, especially the disenfranchised students.

While several districts emerged after one year of being a merged district, I feel like relationships were built among adults and children that were a distant luxury before we all came to the table on behalf of all students. This also helped to unify the message that educators have one primary goal. That goal is to effectively educate all students. The new space also evolved to address issues around class and economics hidden deeply in the cultures of both districts.

In the field of public education for the past 20 years, my roles have included teacher, assistant principal, district staff development coordinator, principal, principal supervisor assistant superintendent of academics, director for outreach, family and community engagement, and most recently, strategic leadership development. These experiences have allowed you to serve in spaces and places as a contributing change agent. My philosophy is inclusive of an unwavering commitment to assist in creating the best teaching and learning environments by ensuring opportunities for academic, social, and emotional success for all students. This is accomplished through clearly stating expectations, creating innovative plans, providing necessary resources, and analyzing data to make informed decisions. I honestly believe the success of an organization, department or individual school is accomplished through the collective efforts of families, teachers, coaches, staff, and administrators working collaboratively with on behalf of all children.

RECOMMENDATIONS FOR CURRENT AND FUTURE LEADERS

Poor parents are depending on educators to make the best decision for them, fully trusting that we are working on their behalf for their children. By creating a plan to navigate the seen and unseen roadblocks that our students and families face, you assume the roles of advocate and educator that will ensure equity and access for all students assigned to your hand as a leader.

As leaders it is not an option to allow atmospheres that bows to the comfort of adults at the expense of our students. Urban children can never choose their teachers, but leaders are in control of who we allow to remain in our schools and classrooms. As urban school leaders we have to make difficult decisions that favor the child, in the midst of opposition or even potential criticism.

The task of serving in education as a leader is a momentous assignment. With the current landscape in education, we have several areas to consider in order to truly experience sustainable success. While never easy, threats can certainly not be ignored. Threats to safety and the academic success of students are an unavoidable priority. When this is consistently addressed, other themes will emerge naturally that will head to future success. Never ignore the hard assignments!

Finally, what seems like the greatest failure always redirects your path and ultimately leads you to greater success. Quitting is not an option when the goal is to guide the next generation to have true access to a future that intentionally includes them!

CHAPTER 12

INNER-CITY PUBLIC SCHOOL'S STILL WORK

How One Principal's Life Is Living Proof

Mateen A. Diop

In 1989, the epic movie *Lean on Me* was released. This film chronicled the leadership of an enigmatic high school principal (Joe Clark) and his efforts to transform an inner-city high school (Eastside High) in Patterson New Jersey. Portrayed by Oscar-winner Morgan Freeman, the story begins with the ouster of the principal Joe Clark. The scene was tense as Mr. Clark addressed several school board members and the superintendent on the proposed transformation of Eastside High. The school board had designs on reconfiguring the school, but Mr. Clark vehemently opposed the plans. For his efforts, he was removed as the principal and reassigned to a teaching position in a suburban school. After several years, faded transformation plans resulting in years of decay and neglect. Feeling pressure from the local community to revive the school, the Mayor summoned the Superintendent Dr. William Napier (played by Robert Guillaume), to address the conditions at Eastside high and to provide solutions. Dr. Napier, with a clairvoyant stare toward the Mayor, had in mind the perfect solution.

Purveyors of Change: School Leaders of Color Share Narratives of Student, School, and Community Success, pp. 109–116
Copyright © 2021 by Information Age Publishing
All rights of reproduction in any form reserved.

The Mayor could sense that Dr. Napier's tentative solution would not be a popular decision. Nonetheless, the Mayor correctly read Dr. Napier's gaze to name Joe Clark the new principal at Eastside High. "Not that animal," the Mayor extolled. However, even the Mayor knew that aggressive leadership was needed if Eastside High were to succeed.

The next scene portrayed Mr. Clark entering school on the first day amazed at what he saw. Walking the halls to the tune of "Welcome to the Jungle" by the rock group Guns N' Roses, Mr. Clark witnessed graffiti on the walls, students smoking and dealing drugs. He saw violence of all sorts and perhaps the lowest graduation rate and state performance he had ever witnessed. The theme of the movie centered around his goal of increasing student performance on the state assessments. Assessed in reading and math, only 20% of Eastside High students had ever achieved a minimum passing score (70%).

I have been in the field of education for 21 years, serving at every level of from pre–K to college. My career began as a middle school teacher and coach. After five years in the classroom, I was named dean of instruction at an elementary school, then assistant principal at the middle school level and finally principal at the elementary level. After six years as an elementary principal, I began to realize that there was more I needed to do in the realm of education. I resigned my position as principal and wrote my first book entitled *Inner City Public School's Still Work, How One Principal's Life is Living Proof* (Authorhouse, 2012). I did not know how long I would remain away from public education, but after one year, I was asked to return to my school district as the director of instructional technology. I served in that role for one year when I was asked again to serve as the chief operating officer of the San Antonio Independent School District—formally titled executive director of special projects and partnerships. In that role, I served as the superintendent's liaison in all matters related to the community and the school district. Once again, after one year, I was asked to serve as the assistant superintendent of Campus Administration.

I thrived in all those central office roles and became comfortable leading an entire school district of roughly 53,000 students. I mentored and coached principals, teachers, and department heads. I founded the Young Men's Leadership Academy, St. Philip's Early College High School, CAST (Center for Applied Science and Technology) Tech High School and was honored to serve on several local, state and federal committees, addressing everything from student attendance to teacher recruitment. After making one last stop in central office as the deputy chief information officer, an opportunity was offered to me— being the principal of Sam Houston High School.

Honestly, when first asked I was bit insulted. I thought to myself, why am I being asked to return to a campus level position, when I have proven my ability to lead at the district level? Sam Houston high school is an inner-city high school, with an enrollment of roughly 1,300 students, and almost a mirror image of Eastside High. Early in my career, I did have aspirations of leading Sam Houston, but as I served at the central office level, the thought of returning to a campus-based position faded. Although feeling defamed, there was an aspect of leading Sam Houston that I could not shake—besides the school being located in the neighborhood where I grew up, and I authored a book on the effectiveness of inner-city schools! I likened my selection as principal to a story in the Bible (Ezekiel 37:1-4), where the Lord commands Ezekiel to go down to a graveyard and speak to dead bones. Ezekiel is commanded to hear the Word of the Lord and talk to the bones. He was asked, "Can these bones live?" As Ezekiel followed God's instructions, the bones began to shake and awaken as they arose from the grave. I am no prophet, and I do not profess to be a biblical scholar by any stretch of the imagination; but, that scripture resonated and continues to resonate in my mind. I eventually accepted the offer to lead Sam Houston, and upon my first day of school, all I could hear was that song playing in my ear "Welcome to the Jungle."

Using a metaphor such as "jungle" to describe an educational setting may sound rather harsh, but one thing about the real-life "jungle," there is an established order- a hierarchy of sorts. All species in the jungle follow a prescribed path of existence—almost like a blueprint. You will never see fish climbing trees or lions swimming in the ocean. In the animal kingdom, the order is maintained and respected. The animal in the jungle that I liken to leadership is the Lion. In Bishop T. D. Jakes's (2014) book *Instinct*, he describes his participation in an African safari. Jakes mentioned how in Africa it is you who are locked in cages as you travel the African landscape. The tour guide protects you from the animals. Unlike a zoo, where the animals are caged; on an African safari, it is YOU who are caged. But, Jakes mentions, of all the animals in the jungle, it is the lion that is dubbed the king of all species. Even though the lion (says Jakes) is not the fastest or the strongest, the lion has an air of confidence that frightens all the other animals into submission. Not unlike school leadership, the principal is not the strongest, tallest, or smartest in the building. However, the building principal has to lead with the confidence of a lion and establish that they are the instructional leaders on their campus. The principal sets the tone charts the course and leads the visioning process. There is a compliment to be labeled a "jungle," at least that is how I made sense of my new sur- roundings at Sam Houston high school.

The metaphorical description of my surroundings as a "jungle" offer substantial evidence that the first trait needed to lead a high school of any size efficiently is ORDER. During my first meeting of the administrative team, I tried to read the tension in the room. I knew there were at least two staff members not chosen for the position sitting around the table.

I made the intentional choice of keeping one on staff as I transitioned into my new role. The thinking was that I would need their experience and leadership to help me navigate the waters of high school leadership. Although I heard rumors about the culture and climate of Sam Houston, nothing could have prepared me for what I was about to witness. ORDER is necessary at the outset and is shaped during team conversations about the vision and direction the school will be led. I sat quietly as my team discussed challenges in the past and their ideas of success. This being my first year, I did not have too much to offer as I needed to witness how the school was operating. We discussed the master schedule, and I was asked my preference for creating the plan. As I mentioned, I was new to high school, so I did not have an educated decision. I asked them what worked in the past and how they thought we could best achieve success. After listening and consulting with a few principal colleagues, I made our final decisions regarding the master schedule.

Our school district pushed the establishment of small learning communities (SLCs), but my team explained that the concept was not used in the past. Since I never created an SLC and was not sure how an SLC operated, I succumbed to their decision NOT to build SLCs. Unlike a professional learning community (PLC), where teachers are grouped according to a content area. SLCs are arranged according to student interests (Allensworth & Easton, 2007), and since I had not met the students nor my staff, I figured the best course was to rely on their judgment. I would soon learn a valuable lesson on leadership—if you are walking into unchartered waters, surround yourself with innovative thinkers, ones who accept challenges, but most of all, are driven to succeed in all facets of their lives.

Although ORDER is the first trait identified as necessary to lead a high school; not too far behind is that of creating a high functioning CULTURE and STRATEGY. In a *Forbes* magazine article entitled "Does Culture Trump Strategy?" Myatt (2019) offered an opposing view to the euphemism of culture eating strategy for breakfast. Myatt asserts that creating a healthy culture is a matter of making it a focal point within the corporate values, vision, mission, and strategy. I too was of the mindset that a sound academic strategy would eventually fade without focusing on culture. My area superintendent was an absolute whiz at identifying the elements needed to succeed academically. However, I knew the commitment to change the culture was solely in my hands. My initial plan was to start with changing the culture followed by a sound academic strategy. It was not long before I realized that (CULTURE and STRATEGY) were not competing terms, but in fact, both are essential elements of a high functioning high school. As the beginning of the school year approached, my learning curve was steep. I had to adjust my thinking back to the daily grind of being a principal. In a central office role, you can become passive when making decisions.

Far too often, as I attended meetings, the outcomes seemed to be "we can implement next year." I knew the people sitting around those tables had never served in campus positions or were so far removed from campus life that no sense of urgency existed in their collective thinking. As the leader of a high school, next year did not exist until "next year." Forced to be in the moment, the lives of my students could not wait until next year. Proactive decisions had to be made.

After establishing ORDER and identifying the current CULTURE and STRATEGIES necessary for success, DATA ANALYSIS was the next essential ingredient. In a high school, there are many data points needed to establish a clear vision for success. To identify state assessments as a clarion call, was too linear to achieve the results I envisioned. To focus on STRATEGY, we had to center on instructional rigor, student schedules, attendance, and teacher professional development. To affect CULTURE, we had to target to teachers and student apathy, parental engagement, and school pride. One of the significant emphasis my team alerted me to was the student's disengagement from school. This disengagement was evidenced by student's walking the halls during instructional time; the student's skipping school, teacher absences, and our historically low student performance on state assessments (State of Texas Assessment of Academic Readiness [STAAR], Advanced Placement scores and national assessments such as the SAT and ACT). After pouring through hours of data, I realized that my teachers did not suffer from lack of trying. They were hard workers and wanted our students to succeed. Our data resembled that of most inner-city school districts. The graduation requirements for Texas students is somewhat strenuous. Students must earn 26-course credits, pass five STAAR (exams in English I and II, biology, U.S. History, and Algebra 1. Students must also have at least a 90% school attendance rate. If any of those requirements are not met, students will not receive a high school diploma. Of particular interest to me was our student's performance on the English I and II assessment. In 2016, 70% of our students taking the English I assessment DID NOT MEET standard (58% for first-time testers).

Our English II assessments did not fare any better, as 70% did not meet standard there either. But, more concerning; there is a level passing rated as "Mastered." To score "Mastered," this means students have demonstrated college readiness skills. On both exams, only five students total achieved such a distinction. It was no secret that our challenge would be strengthening the reading and writing abilities of our students. To effectively challenge and increase our student's mastery of reading and writing, we had to do what Phillip C. Schlechty recommended—*working* on the work. Schlechty (2002) outlined a motivational framework for improving student performance by improving the quality of schools designed for students. My teachers desired to achieve, but our student's failure to produce lead me to the next ingredient for efficiently running a high school—STUDENT ENGAGEMENT. It was interesting having conversations with new teachers about their university certification process. What I observed in the classroom was that they were teaching as I taught 20 years ago. They loved their content, but most were not skilled at transferring that knowledge to our students. Most teachers (new and veteran) all suffered from the "sage on the stage" mentality. They talked and talked, while students walked and walked (the halls). Whenever we redirected a student back to class, I felt terrible for the students because I knew the rigor level needed to be increased in the classroom to engage the students.

Nine weeks passed, and it was our first professional development since the school year began. I created sessions for teachers to attend, taught by our staff. As teachers transitioned from meeting to meeting, I took the time just to walk the halls and get a better understanding of the geography of the building. Since I began the position the previous summer, I did not have much time to gather my thoughts and get a sense of the task at hand. As I strolled up and down the halls, I thought of students walking the building, students not engaged in the classroom and the number of teacher absences per day. I am an absolute believer in the power that education has to disrupt poverty, so this apathy toward learning was foreign to me.

For my learners to succeed, I knew that change was needed now. Questions popped into my head such as: (1) "How can we engage students in the educational process?" (2) "How can we create an environment where students will want to attend school?" It was then the idea hit me! The next ingredient in efficiently running a high school are positive student RELATIONSHIPS. Students are resistant to staying in class and dropping out because no one has taken a vested interest in THAT student. I pondered how I could somehow make the classrooms and even the whole school seem smaller, allowing all of us to give the students more personalized attention. If students knew that we cared about them (individually) and wanted them to graduate, then maybe they would put forth more effort in the classroom.

Later the notion of SLSs became clear. Daniel Pink (2006), in his best-selling book entitled *Drive*, wrote about large companies such as Walmart and Apple appearing to be small. So small, those companies wanted to be considered neighborhood stores. How could a behemoth like Apple seem to a consumer to be a little store? Apple's strategy was to promise personalized customer service. If a defective product needed to be replaced, how could Apple guarantee it would be returned in less than three days? Apple products are mainly created in China, so if my iPad needed repair, how could I return it to Apple, send it to China, then send back to me in 3-days? To fulfill the 3-day promise, Apple created repair centers in all their regional hubs. In reality, the devices were not sent to China for repair;

the machines were sent to the nearest center, repaired, and sent back to the customer.

The concept of an SLC can have similar results! Since relationships are an integral part of the learning process, if students are surrounded by committed, caring adults, positive academic achievement is the outcome. As we began planning for the next semester, I asked my staff again to explain the concept of an SLC. A SLC, also referred to as a *school-within-a-school*, is a school organizational model that is an increasingly common form of a learning environment in American secondary schools to subdivide large school populations into smaller, autonomous groups of students and teachers. I started to envision our second-semester grouping our school into a small learning community. If you have spent any time in a high school, then you would know that decision would require a complete revamping of our master schedule.

Teachers heard whispers of my proposal, and the wave of concern began. I was contacted by the teacher alliance, department chairs and parents. The idea of changing the master schedule mid-year terrified my staff. I have never been to shy away from a challenge, but, since this seemed the proverbial line-in-the-sand for my teachers, I thought it best to leave our current master schedule in place and make minor changes in teacher assignments as needed. The thought still resonated with me as to why my administrative team did not want to institute SLCs during the initial creation of the master schedule.

The final ingredient, and perhaps the most important to efficiently leading an inner-city high school is to surround students with COMMITTED, CARING ADULTS. Schleck (2002) stated that although teachers are leaders, it is much more important that teachers provide quality experiences for students and that they (students) learn what they are intended to absorb. Conducting teacher appraisals, we assess the teachers and their ability to perform. However, we never determine what the students are learning. The teachers are required to complete specific tasks (establish clear learning objectives, differentiate instruction), and they are worth as teachers are rated accordingly. Whenever I visit classrooms, after visually searching the class the clear learning objectives, my next strategy is to ask the students what they are working on.

If the learning objectives are clear, the students will be able to articulate what it is they are doing. Many times, when I question students, I hear vague answers such as "We are doing this worksheet." Upon further questioning, they finally say "We are doing this because the teacher gave us the assignment." In a classroom of committed, caring adults, the teacher ensures the students understand what and why they are completing each assignment. When asking a student in committed teachers' classrooms, what they are doing, that student will respond with "We are studying and identifying the causes of the Revolutionary War." When I hear those answers, the natural questions flow—"What is the Revolutionary War?" In the literature of America's Promise, they outline five essential ingredients to the success of American children, and committed, caring adults is mentioned as critical. They measure "caring adults" not only by good relationships between parents and their children, but also by the involvement of others in school and through their communities who can guide, assist, and mentor young people toward bright futures. What is more, young people actively want this developmental resource. More than one-half of young people in the 2006 America's Promise *Every Child, Every Promise* report said that they look for advice and help from adults on doing well in school, relationships with friends, jobs and careers, and college. Furthermore, more than 40% of the young people ages 8 through 21 said they want more adults in their lives to whom they can turn for help (America's Promise Alliance, 2019). During a recent roundtable discussion with a group of my top 10 seniors, they were asked to name what they like most about high school, and an area that can be improved. After going through a litany of ways I could improve the school, the one factor mentioned as the highlight of their day, is when the find teachers who care about them. I extol my teachers that caring is free. I challenge each of them to look beyond the rough exterior of some of our students and find that seed buried within each of them. I ask them to provide that seed with ample nourishment, and just like the flower the seed will bloom with the right amount of sunshine and water, so too will our students blossom when we plant the seeds of success in their mind, water them with love and encouragement, then they will soon return to our lives, that which the plants and flowers provide to the world.

REFERENCES

Allensworth, E. M., & Easton, J. Q. (2007). *What matters for staying on-track and graduating in Chicago public high schools*. Consortium on Chicago School Research at the University of Chicago.

America's Promise Alliance. (2006). *Every child every promise*. https://www.americaspromise.org/sites/default/files/d8/Every%20Child%20Every%20Promise%20-%20Full%20Report.pdf

America's Promise Alliance. (2019). *Caring adults*. https://www.americaspromise.org/promise/caring-adults

Jakes, T. D. (2014). *Instinct. The power to unleash your inborn drive*. Faith Words.

Myatt, M. (2019). Culture versus strategy: What's more important. *Forbes Magazine*. https://www.forbes.com/sites/mikemyatt/2012/05/29/culture-vs-strategy-whats-more-important/#224b012e72f0

Schlechty, P. C. (2002). *Working on the work: An action plan for teachers, principals, and superintendents*. Jossey-Bass.

Pink, D. H. (2009). *Drive: The surprising truth about what motivates us*. Riverhead Books.

PART IV

SOCIAL JUSTICE LEADERSHIP

CHAPTER 13

TALKING BACK

Two Leaders Dialogue About Leading
While Black for Social Justice

Jamel Adkins-Sharif and Natalie D. Lewis

This dialogue began as two members of a graduate student panel on education leadership discussing similar research interests and roles as school leaders. As we shared, we began to see through-lines in our leadership priorities and in the theoretical lens through which we analyzed dilemmas in our respective schools. Further, we share the concern that the lived experience of Black school leaders is a unique perspective largely absent in our understanding of leadership dilemmas facing public schools, specifically those impacting children and communities of color. Critical race theory compels us to create counter stories that speak to our own realities, as answer back and disbelief to the notion that there is one objective view on school leadership or its theoretical undergirding. We reject as singular the reality defined by white male perspectives on leading, teaching and learning (Capper, 2012; Delgado, 1989). This essay presents our reality of urban school administration, informed by our experience of being Black in a racialized society that has historically underserved Black children. Jamel

Adkins-Sharif leads an elementary school in Boston, Massachusetts; Natalie Lewis is a principal of a middle school in Denver, Colorado. Social justice leadership theory demands that we keep at the center of our practice issues of marginalization in schools, and actively dismantle barriers to equity and justice (Theoharis, 2007). In an effort to create our counter narrative, and fight inequity, we endeavor to engage in dialogue as two Black educators, centering our experiences in leading schools. We offer reflections, recount our stories, and hope the reader derives benefit from our lessons learned.

We strive daily to live a leadership and scholarship praxis grounded in social justice. We champion the voice and lived experience of communities of color, and in particular look to elevate and illuminate the genius in Black children. We have overcome obstacles, suffered setbacks, and tried to keep our eyes on the prize of justice, empowerment, and equity in all things school. In our dialogue, we will discuss our experiences centered around a few research questions.

WHAT ARE SOME OF THE CHALLENGES THAT YOU'VE FACED DURING YOUR TIME AS A BLACK SCHOOL LEADER?

Jamel: One of the challenges I constantly face is striking the right balance between matters of equity in pedagogy and climate. Meaning, there is often pressure to prioritize dilemmas of school culture over of instruction. My approach is often to show that we are capable of working on these areas simultaneously, and that ultimately our locus of control centers on what we can change about ourselves, namely the quality of learning experiences we plan and prepare for our youngsters. I ask my staff questions like, what opportunities are you providing for student leadership? How often has a student taught or co-taught a concept in your class? Where is the culture of your students reflected in your classroom, the conversations you choose to hold, or the books available to read? How are the issues of importance in your students' communities showing up in your daily instruction? What structured opportunities exist for discussing, debating, and building on ideas, since these exercises are not only critical for communication and schema development? Meaning, Black and Brown folks tend to have well developed and sophisticated oral communication strategies and skills in their home environments, and the associated neural pathways are primed for further development in well planned classrooms, so use them! (Hammond, 2015).

As a principal of an elementary school in Boston, all around me are instances where students do not experience sustained success. I am struck by the frequency in which opportunities to teach are missed and instead refashioned as instances to correct. I can reflect on a group of third grade boys who constantly found themselves in trouble, particularly during lunch and recess. At first glance, it can seem like just run of the mill young male aggression getting the best of them; probe deeper, and there are issues of cultural mismatch, i.e., White teachers, routinely exaggerating misbehaviors as being more egregious than they actually are. Did the boys fight, or was there simply shoving and inappropriate language? Did he throw the chair or knock it over and cause it to slide across the floor? Did the teacher not provide an escape "route" for the overwhelmed student, and as a consequence, set the conditions for that child to shove them out of the way? And am I really expected to code an incident between a 30-year-old and a 5-year-old as an assault by the latter? The Black leader for social justice understands that daily occurrences like these, if improperly handled, begin to paint a profile of dangerous assaultive children of color, versus children for whom adult interventions are thus far inadequate or inappropriate. Such conclusions play into stereotypes about Black children and tempt a perspective that they must be controlled (Yosso, 2006). This then becomes the starting point in discussions about this/these child/children; they cease to be primarily students to be taught, but behaviors to be regulated. As an administrator, I scrutinize those incident reports for subjectivity. You must insist that teachers are the first contact between the school and families, and that reporting negative incidents should not constitute the initial contact. And you must convey these expectations to your leadership team. Whenever possible, you must bring the discussion back to the prime directive, that of providing an education. I communicate about teaching and learning as a comprehensive experience, involving teacher and student alternating in both roles. A deficit mindset begins from the presumption that only the child has something to learn, to behave, follow rules, take directions, compute. Asset thinking and growth mindset embrace the idea that there are lessons yet revealed to the teacher, about students' culture, or learning preferences, or the way their parents show involvement. There must be discovery on both sides. What's been your experience?

Natalie: My past experience as an assistant principal in particular, has been one in which issues of discipline and behavior all come to me and I'm expected to mediate if not "fix" those that cannot abide by the school-wide expectations. As a Black leader, I feel charged to constantly look deeper at concerns and issues to discover what might be root causes below the surface. After digging further through classroom observations and discussions with students and teachers, I realize that a significant number of teachers are not adhering to each step of our school's discipline ladder. This leads to inconsistencies of expectations amongst students and for students from class to class. In my former role as assistant principal of a middle school in Denver, I strive to ensure that I've woven foundations of equity and social justice into the school culture systems that I've designed.

For me this means creating a system that limits the potential for subjectivity. Numerous scholars have detailed how Black and Brown children (Skiba, 2015; Noguera, 2014; Lhamon & Samuel, 2014) are disproportionately impacted by subjective adherence and/or enforcement of discipline. So, the charge as a Black school administrator leading school culture means that one must be absolutely clear and consistent around the messaging, implementation and adjustments of the system.

In effort to ensure consistency, I practice with my staff on ways to effectively implement the school discipline ladder with equity and consistency. Initially my efforts and the hard work of planning is well received. We collectively discuss and brainstorm as a team our vision of a strong school culture. In order to be clear with a shared vision for a strong school culture, I dig deeply to surface each member's mental models (Senge, 2009). In hopes of surfacing and bringing transparency about the significance of mental models, I push members and provide scenarios of challenging school cultures. After some hesitance staff begins to share and we start the year with a solid, collective vision for school culture.

Like most schools, we hold professional development right before the start of the school year and hope that the planning and practice of the summer will be enough to launch a successful school year. As a team, I believe we created a shared vision and that everyone has a clear understanding of how to utilize the systems of school culture. However, at about week three it becomes clear that bias and lack of experience with students from different cultural backgrounds becomes a challenge for teachers and their use of systems, as comments begin to rise about whether or not our school culture systems can be effective with "those" kids. Difficult at times, the role of assistant principal stated that your charge is support to the vision of the principal. This becomes challenging when they acquiesce to the pleas of teachers with stricter, more visible treatment of the students that look like you and that you absolutely want to protect by treating them equitably and just.

WHAT DOES IT MEAN TO BE A BLACK SCHOOL LEADER WHEN LEADING COMMUNITIES OF COLOR?

Natalie: Often Black and Brown students and subsequently their families have negative relationships with schools. These negative relationships stem from a variety of origins, most of which include the inability for non-People of Color, majority White teachers and administrators to build sustainable and authentic relationships with Black and Brown students and their families. Whether from painful classroom experiences to inadequate and unfairly biased disciplinary actions experienced by students, the impact to students and families do not change. Black and Brown students and their families often feel marginalized, isolated, and more importantly disconnected from their schools. This feeling and its impact is especially significant to Black School Leaders, as they are often the "bridge" that connects school to Black and Brown students and families.

Jamel: We must leverage families, in particular Black and Brown families, as resources and the first places for support of students. In reflecting on a recent conversation with a parent whose child is struggling, it was necessary to break some barriers to communication. This parent had come to distrust schools because her only experience was to be hauled in for disciplinary hearings. A pattern of avoidance and denial became her standard response to contact from the school. In a nearly one-hour phone conversation, I had to mostly listen, to inconsistencies and projection of fault, before the issues were finally revealed. Her son had difficulty focusing, was consequently falling behind academically, and she didn't know what to do about it. As we processed the beginning of a plan and some next steps, I realized this was the mother's way of protecting her child and herself. So often in past experience, caregivers of color are not heard, or their views dismissed; when they do get an ear, it's sometimes their only opportunity to unload. The caring Black educator for social justice must recognize the difference between survival and obfuscation and see hope and promise through the clutter of fear and distrust.

HOW DO YOU PROVIDE SPACE AND AGENCY WITHIN YOUR SCHOOL FOR FAMILIES OF COLOR?

Jamel: I have long believed that an informed, voiced, and culturally valued parent/caregiver community is a critical factor in creating both just and better performing schools for our children. I am working now to develop spaces for authentic family voice in decisions made at the school. A challenge for me currently is that the majority of my students are from homes where caregivers are primarily Spanish speaking. This means I am simultaneously trying to demystify the policies and language of "school" while not being proficient in the home language of my various families. I, therefore, position myself as co-learner; the patience and humility required to learn Spanish and be a more effective communicator to my families informs my efforts to familiarize them with school governing structures, visioning, and instructional improvement efforts. Again, broadly speaking, we are all learning.

Natalie: I too, place a huge value in allowing families to be the first advocate and greatest source of knowledge on who and what is best for their children. I've spent a significant portion of my time as a leader, convincing teachers and other members of staff that families should be notified immediately when there are concerns about child. I believe that this notification should happen from something as small as a in the classroom misstep to a concern regarding academic progress. I push the staff that I work with to move beyond their beliefs regarding families and a student's at-home experience. I've created scripts and role played with staff on how to make phone calls home. I vividly remember having several mediation meetings with a Black mother that was upset that her daughter was having behavioral challenges in her class and she had not received one phone call from the teacher! I then approached the teacher and asked why he had not called the parent. His faced immediately flushed red with embarrassment and he grew very quiet. I raised my voice and snapped my neck (in my best Sistah-gurl) and asked him if it was because she spoke like this. He lowered his eyes and nodded his head yes.

Jamel: I'll bet he was surprised.

Natalie: I then explained to him that it was essential that he immediately contact families to inform them of everything concerning their children. And that it is his responsibility to understand that people communicate differently than him and that he should not assign judgement or value to different forms of communication. I knew that in that moment I had to not only correct the misjudgment, but also provide him with tools that he could utilize when faced in other similar circumstances. So, I practiced with him using role play, how he would call the mother to discuss her daughter's behavior and repair their broken relationship.

WHAT DOES YOUR LEADERSHIP MEAN TO YOU AND HOW DO OTHERS RESPOND TO YOUR LEADERSHIP?

Natalie: Our truth, doing this work is hard. The complexity of its exhaustive nature is multifaceted. First, as a Black school leader we never underestimate the significance and charge of the role that we are filling. We are often the only or few in our position, so there is a delicate balance that consistently must be maintained. As one of the few, we stand and speak for the voiceless, forgotten and not considered. This means that we can easily become targeted, misjudged, and misunderstood. In order to make this work more sustainable and our commitment strong, I believe that it is essential to surround yourself with a "squad" you can trust. Your squad should know what you stand for, can represent, and speak for your values even when you're not present and should share your deep belief in equity and fighting for social justice.

Jamel: I would say my leadership is meant to make visible barriers to equity. Whether it is race, gender, ability, poverty, bring it to light. I seek to provide data, trends, anecdotes, and ask what we think this means? What explains it? And when all roads point to structural roots, systems, policies, practices that have the effect of producing the same limiting result, I call them for what they are, and ask others to do the same, as the first step in their elimination. Second, Black leadership to me means to simultaneously lead your school while advocating for families; often it's the same families whose children have been historically ignored. They are the ones whose voices have been left out, like ours on leading. They are the ones who need the key to the code, and the space to claim their space. I expect others to respond in ways indicative of where they situate themselves in the struggle for social justice. If oblivious to the centrality of this struggle in education, perhaps it is predictable that they respond with shock, dismay, and defensiveness. Those who would focus primarily on symptoms of the opportunity gap, persistent negative outcomes for children of color, begin and end their analysis with the targets of a system of oppression, and never the system itself. Illuminating a dynamic and structure rendered invisible can be destabilizing to hegemony. And yet shedding such light also creates space for those marginalized, to recognize and claim their power to enact change. Such is the response we tend to experience from families of color; an affirmation that their instincts are correct, that neither their children not their culture are the problem, and that solutions exist within the possibilities of their collective wisdom and action.

REFERENCES

Capper, C. A. (2015). The 20th-year anniversary of critical race theory in education: Implications for leading to eliminate racism. *Educational Administration Quarterly, 51*(5), 791–833. https://doi.org/10.1177/0013161x15607616

Delgado, R. (1989). Storytelling for oppositionists and others: A plea for narrative. *Michigan Law Review, 87*(8), 2411. https://doi.org/10.2307/1289308

Hammond, Z., Jackson, Y. (2015) *Culturally responsive teaching and the brain: Promoting authentic engagement and rigor among culturally and linguistically diverse students.* SAGE.

Lhamon, C., & Samuels, J., (2014). OCR guidance letter to colleagues. http://www2. ed.gov/about/offices/list/ocr/letters/colleague-201401-title-vi.html

Noguera, P. A. (2014). Urban schools and the Black male "challenge." *Handbook of Urban Education*, 114–128.

Senge, P. M. (2009) *The fifth discipline: the art and practice of the learning organization.* Doubleday

Skiba R. J. (2015) Interventions to address racial/ethnic disparities in school discipline: Can systems reform be race-neutral? In R. Bangs & L. Davis (Eds.), *Race and social problems.* Springer.

Theoharis, G. (2007). Social justice educational leaders and resistance: Toward a theory of social justice leadership. *Educational Administration Quarterly, 43*(2), 221–258.

Yosso, T. J. (2006). Whose culture has capital? A critical race theory discussion of community cultural wealth. *Race Ethnicity and Education, 8*(1), 69–91.

CHAPTER 14

LEADING AGAINST
ANTI-BLACKNESS

Floyd Cobb

As I sit down to write this chapter, and I ponder on the state of mind I had as a graduate student in my educational leadership program, I likely would not believe what I am about to say. Even though these words are my own, I am certain that I would have assumed the things that follow in the subsequent pages of this chapter were wrong. I would have assumed that what I am about to say was a mistake, or the experiences were somehow aberrant and distinct from what I would experience. However, as I write this now with more of my career behind me than ahead of me, I feel an intense responsibility to speak to you about the realities of *our* experiences leading schools, even if I would not have fully understood this at the time.

Now, if you are anything like I was as a graduate student you feel ready to lead a school, you have probably immersed yourself in the study of change theory, learned everything you could organizational culture, and are well versed in the most current research related to school improvement. Like me you are probably fixated on eradicating racial disparities in the many ways they show up in public education. I was self-assured in my ability to achieve what had never been done because unlike a number of my colleagues who often speak of a desire to achieve greater equity within our

Purveyors of Change: School Leaders of Color Share Narratives of Student, School, and Community Success, pp. 127–131
Copyright © 2021 by Information Age Publishing

schools, I understood the research and could bring together their passion and my knowledge to achieve the impossible. I was going to be the one to succeed where my other colleagues could not. All I needed was my chance to lead and an opportunity to apply what I had learned. I knew as soon as I was afforded the freedom to lead a school in the way that I knew how, together we could be the ones to bring about educational equity within our school.

However, it was not long after I entered into leadership I realized the shortsightedness and naiveté of my thinking. While my professional preparation was solid and my understanding of how research could be applied in schools, I failed to consider the depths to which countless assumptions about anti-Blackness remained so deeply enmeshed into public schooling and most importantly into the problem that I had committed myself to solve (Dumas, 2016).

Looking back on it now I feel somewhat foolish because the signs were all there and I just failed to see them. I wanted to continue to believe that once one arrived in a leadership position that he or she was judged not by the color of one's skin but by the content of one's character. All one needed to do was ascend and earn a position in school leadership and then the negative assumptions would be a thing of the past. I needed that myth to be true even though somewhere buried in the depths of my soul, I knew the story that I was telling myself was nothing more than just that.

Now when I speak of anti-Blackness, I want to be certain to recognize it as a construct that is far more sophisticated, nuanced, and targeted than the everyday racism to which we are all familiar. Certainly, most honest individuals can identify deliberate hatred toward groups of people for no other reason than the color of their skin but far fewer number have stopped to interrogate the unquestioned inhumanity that leads to such hatred. It is here where anti-Blackness is applied.

Introduced by Dumas (2016), anti-Blackness is regarded as the accepted and unchallengedc nonhumanness of the Black identity. First established by the legitimized brutality of chattel slavery, only to be furthered by barbaric laws and dehumanizing stereotypes anti-Blackness represents the normative ways in which people of all races (including Black people) have come to show disdain for the Black identity. Viewing it primarily for its role as a commodity, Blackness and most importantly black people are far too often considered undeserving of basic human dignity. It is this very ideology that even to this day leads to never ending debates about the value and worth of Black life. Anti-Blackness is both durable and pervasive creating the very substructure on which racial discrimination rests. Its omnipresence is what places it below the surface and makes it seem barely visible, thus confounding every conversation focused on the pursuit of racial justice.

Therefore, it should not take a giant leap of logic to recognize the historical presence of anti-Blackness in America's public schools. This ideology served as the justification for school-based segregation and it manifests itself in rationalizations for racial disparities in performance and school discipline. Anti-Blackness is the impediment that makes efforts to achieve school equality feel like an unending struggle, impacting students, parents, teachers, and school leaders alike. As an ideology, it cuts across all races and even influences the well-meaning. This is why trying to lead schools equitably while Black is so difficult, because we must contend with the role that anti-Blackness plays; not only in the treatment of the very students we are trying to support but, in the assumptions, that people of all races choose to make about ourselves and our deservingness to occupy roles as school leaders.

Practically speaking, it is the subtleties of anti-Blackness that encourage school cultures to "value diversity," while simultaneously placing conditions on the ways in which those diverse individuals are to act. It is anti-Blackness that encourages the creation of school policies that suspends Black girls for their hairstyle (Bennett, 2017; Kim, 2016). It is anti-Blackness that leads to never-ending arguments justifying dehumanizing literature in English courses (Timpf, 2016). It is anti-Blackness that permits students engaging in a school performance black face (McCray, 2018). It is anti-Blackness that will lead your colleagues to discourage you from challenging these policies and practices that violate the core of your very being.

Ignorance of this simple fact may have been my greatest oversight prior to entering into school leadership. Principally, I was deliberately blind to the ways in which anti-Blackness allowed too many of those with whom I worked to view my racial identity as a form of capital (Leong, 2012). I saw my presence as an effort to create systems to bring out the inherent brilliance of children who looked like me, while others saw my role as nothing more than a commodity to help keep Black children under control (Brockenbrough, 2015).

While I refused to see it at the time, it has become painfully clear to me now, I had at times been exploited for the plausible deniability that numerical diversity offers since they held values different from me about the value and worth of Black children (Cobb, 2017). This despite the fact that I was encouraged to pursue such roles to use my knowledge to support our efforts in the attainment of greater educational equity. Notwithstanding my many talents, there were those who would rather have had me serve a tokenized presence even though that was the furthest thing from my mind. However, this unfortunately again is how the normative function anti-Blackness works, because the perceptions about the value and worth of American Blackness does not cease with assumptions about Black children. It remains a constant presence in the lives of adults.

Now some (even those who are Black) might lead you to believe that there is a way that you can work your identity in such a way where the pressures of anti-Blackness can be avoided, provided you compromise your values related to equity (Carbado & Gulati, 2013). They will be the ones to have you believe that if you "play the game long enough" that a time will come when you will be seen for the person you are, thus giving you permission to be the person that you want to be. But I want to be clear when I tell you this, *that day never arrives*. Compromising your racial identity at the expense of Black children in hopes that one day you will be professionally rewarded is a fool's errand. Moreover, the suggestion that you should do so is nothing more than a manifestation of the power of anti-Blackness.

With all of this written I am sure you are probably asking yourself if I think it is even possible for Black leaders to make an impact. After all, the picture I have painted in the last few pages would seem like an effort to discourage even the most confident of candidates destined for school leadership. So, I would expect you to be asking, where do we go from here? At the risk of being repetitive, I want to restate what I offered at the beginning of this chapter and remind you that we desperately need you. As a fellow Black educational leader, and father of Black children "I need you to hear me say we need you."

However, I have written this chapter from this lens in an effort to remind you that by dedicating yourself to be a leader in this work you can never lose sight that it is not easy and that you have committed yourself to struggle. Your efforts are an attempt to create a public educational system that has never existed. One that sees the full humanity of Black children. So yes, this work is hard! However, as Martin Luther King, Jr. (1967) reminds us "[h]uman progress is neither automatic nor inevitable. Even a superficial look at history reveals that no social advance rolls in on the wheels of inevitability. Every step towards the goal of justice requires sacrifice, suffering, and struggle." Therefore, as we make the conscious choice to engage in this type of justice related work, we all must struggle.

Failure to recognize this fact and its intersecting force of anti-Blackness was a significant mistake that I made early on in my career. This was something that those who came before me were suffering through and I could not see. I have written this chapter in an effort to assist you in not doing the same. The pain I have suffered through my reluctance to accept this fact is something I want none of those who come after me to needlessly have to repeat. While it might seem counterintuitive and hopeless to accept such a reality, it is the recognition and acceptance of that struggle that keep you from wallowing in the deep pits of despair (Cobb, 2017).

James Baldwin (1962/1991) reminds us "[w]e are capable of bearing a great burden, once we discover that the burden is reality and arrive where reality is" (p. 91). Leading against anti-Blackness is that burden and this chapter is my attempt to bring you into that reality. Therefore, I want you to know you are being confronted with that burden that you are not alone and there are countless leaders out there who are standing with you. You signed up for a fight which means that you need to expect to get hit back. Know that sometimes those punches will hurt and might even knock you down, just keep getting back up. We have got work to do!

REFERENCES

Baldwin, J. (1991). *The fire next time*. Vintage. (Original work published 1962)

Bennett, L. (2017, May 19). *Local teen told afro is 'extreme' and can't be worn at school*. WCTV. http://www.wctv.tv/content/news/Local-teen-told-cant-wear-hairstyle-at-school-423232994.html

Brockenbrough, E. (2015). "The discipline stop" Black male teachers and the politics of urban school discipline. *Education and Urban Society*, *47*(5), 499–522.

Carbado, D. W., & Gulati, M. (2013). *Acting white? Rethinking race in post-racial America*. Oxford University Press.

Cobb, F. (2017). *Leading while Black: Reflections on the racial realities of Black school leaders through the Obama era and beyond*. Peter Lang.

Dumas, M. J. (2016). Against the dark: Anti-blackness in education policy and discourse. *Theory into Practice*, *55*(1), 11–19.

Kim, E. (2016, May 5). *Mom wants apology from school after daughter, 9, is sent home because of her hairstyle*. NBC News. https://www.today.com/parents/mom-wants-apology-school-after-daughter-9-sent-home-because-t90956

King, M. L., Jr. (1967, August 16). *Where do we go from here?* http://kingencyclopedia.stanford.edu/encyclopedia/documentsentry/where_do_we_go_from_here_delivered_at_the_11th_annual_sclc_convention/

Leong, N. (2012). Racial capitalism. *Harvard Law Review*, *126*, 2151.

McCray, V. (2018, March 30). *Atlanta charter school apologizes for blackface depiction during student program*. https://www.myajc.com/news/local-education/atlanta-second-graders-blackface-masks-draw-outrage-apology/zHmUEKx5H81hGAZIHLzMxL/

Timpf, K. (2016, Dec. 6). Banning Huck Finn would hurt more than it helps. *The National Review*. https://www.nationalreview.com/2016/12/banning-huckleberry-finn-racial-slurs-virginia-school/

CHAPTER 15

WHEN HEGEMONY, MICROAGGRESSIONS, AND WHITE FRAGILITY UNDERMINE YOUR LEADERSHIP

Raphael Crawford

The role of the P–12 principal has changed significantly, morphing from a site-based operational manager to an instructional expert and educational statistician. While school districts have provided marginal expert training that prepares school leaders for their new role, some building-level leaders have received district resources and supports to combat challenges related to the new role and the continued traditional responsibilities of the principal. Conversely, the challenges associated with the principalship of Black principals are often a unique set of challenges associated with race, attitudes, organizational structure, and policies (Echols, 2006). Given the preponderance of hegemony in American public education, Leaders of Color, and specifically those identified as Black, find themselves in the quagmire of either succumbing to the fragility of White district superiors and school-based subordinates, or boldly creating culturally competent and socially just learning environments that honor Children of Color and

Purveyors of Change: School Leaders of Color Share Narratives of Student, School, and Community Success, pp. 133–138
Copyright © 2021 by Information Age Publishing
133

provides them with the education they deserve. This mental space takes a personal and professional toll on Leaders of Color, a heavy tax not required or paid by their White peers. It is my contention that Leaders of Color must know themselves and their strengths and be personally and professionally grounded enough to withstand the harsh and constant efforts to undermine their leadership.

In my experience, Black principals are almost always assigned to the lowest performing, underresourced, and most challenging schools, usually located in the most impoverished areas. The one time I was assigned to a predominantly White suburban school, I experienced the most overt hostilities and racism of my entire career. I vividly remember the first day I arrived on campus and while unloading boxes from my car, a group of White parents and teachers approached me and stated, "We don't want you here!" That school year was my toughest because not only were most of the faculty and staff unfriendly and racist, but so were many of the students and parents. I constantly faced insubordination and attempts to undermine my work. Complicating matters was the fact that my supervisor undermined everything I tried to get done and worked constantly to destroy my reputation as an educational leader; but, I was compelled to succeed because while there were only a few Black faculty members, staff, and students at the school, I had to fight for them—I knew they were watching me. However, according to Brooks and Watson (2018), the heart of the matter is that the majority of paradigms of school leadership privileges White people in general and White children in particular. My efforts to build culturally competent and inclusive schools and address the needs of struggling children of color have always resulted in personal attacks against me.

During my tenure, I have overcome almost insurmountable job-related personal and professional attacks. Leaders of Color always have their competence challenged, and when their competence is clearly stellar, their character becomes targeted. I learned along the way to command respect, and that as a Black principal I had to use all the might in me to withstand attacks, betrayals, and undermining by superiors and subordinates. Students, especially students of color, had to see me smile and succeed; they had to see me make their schools and learning experiences the absolute best. Because defeat was never an option, I became more focused and resilient. I decided to make that "Black Tax" I had paid provide opportunities for success for my "babies," my young scholars are, indeed, my babies.

Years ago, I was branded a "turnaround" principal, indicating my success at refocusing schools on the brink of state takeover or closure. Through hard work and the personal sacrifices of incredible teachers, school personnel, parents, and students, every school I led met or exceeded achievement score mandates. We were able to drastically decrease out of school suspensions, increased parent engagement, and connect schools with community resources. My leadership resulted in a visit with U.S. President, George H. W. Bush, as well as visits and commendations by former Tennessee Governor Bill Haslam. Though my work has been exemplary, and I have been highly regarded in educational circles, I bear the battle scars of being a Black principal in the south. Accordingly, I offer three general areas:

1. Stand for Students

There is only one way to do the right thing! First and foremost, everything you do must be grounded in the best interests of your students. Leaders of Color must not become dissuaded from doing what is the absolute best for students, especially for Children of Color. Too often school Leaders of Color, give in to the fatigue and ostracism caused by the system of White supremacy, and become purveyors of systemic racism in school districts. The desire for material gains and professional status must never become more important than the work of leading meaningful educational reforms that benefits and evens the playing field for Children of Color. School districts often use threats of job security as a means of breaking and silencing strong Leaders of Color. It is not uncommon for Black principals to be demoted, fired, or forced into retirement when they fight for Black students and schools.

Leaders of Color must boldly address the systemic White fragility that disrupts schools and learning and maintains a system of public education that fails Children of Color. Leaders of Color, especially those identified as Black, are generally labeled as "angry Black women" or "angry Black men" whenever they confront White subordinates or superiors with facts related to their job-related behaviors. "White tears" from a subordinate, especially a White female always equals trouble for the Black leader, no matter the infraction or detriment to students. A homogenous teaching pool creates a context for schools where White teachers, particularly White women, are situated as the norm. Therefore, White teachers' sense-making around issues of racism and social justice can be limited when they are not exposed or simply refuse to engage in issues of difference, privilege, and oppression, even when such issues directly affect their professional roles and influence on the students with whom they work (Patton & Jordan, 2017).

One must be prepared to have decisions challenged, to be second-guessed, and to be confronted by subordinates and superiors often. There is a prevailing thought that Leaders of Color are only hired based on skin color, and somehow are not as smart or prepared as their White counterparts. That became a driving force for me and kept me outperforming my peers with every expectation for my schools. Likewise, the belief exists that Black principals are not good enough to lead predominantly White schools. In my experience, White parents tended to present a definite challenge to my authority and leadership.

Leaders of Color must be at the forefront of recruitment efforts for teachers and school personnel who reflect their student body. As a principal, I often made it a point to forge relationships with local university schools of education to share my needs for teachers of color. The persistence of White-staffed segregated schools for impoverished Black communities is predictable and does predictable damage to students, families, and communities (Milligan & Howley, 2015).

2. Stand for the Voiceless

As a Leader of Color, one must be committed to the cause of social justice, we do not have the luxury of ignoring social injustices in the communities we serve. Students of Color, especially those identified as Black face significant obstacles in P–12 schools, and school leaders must be willing to ensure that these children are protected from excessive abuses based on racial stereotypes. While much attention has been given to the number of Black boys streamlined to special education programs with lowered expectations, Whiteness, White middle-class values, and Eurocentric Western notions of femininity place Black girls at high-risk of being overly identified as in need of special education interventions, and under identified in referrals for gifted education (Evans-Winters, 2014).

Be it suspension rates, absenteeism, disruptive behaviors, or signs of mental decline, Leaders of Color must be on the forefront of service provision that promotes school attendance and success. That too, in my experience, comes with resistance and micro aggressions from both subordinates and superiors. However, school leaders must accept the challenge of being the advocate for each child entrusted to his or her care. Leaders and Teachers of Color are often the only voice our babies may have.

Standing against microaggressions from subordinates and superiors takes a personal toll on the school leader, who must function at the highest levels while often feeling at their lowest. Microaggressions may take the form of verbal and nonverbal insults, hostilities, derogatory remarks, and unkind facial gestures. Often superiors may express lowered expectations of the leader and his or her capability to lead, or surprise that students of the school have done well. Almost always are those behaviors followed by a forced and veiled apology.

I often share with Leaders of Color that it is not possible to be all things to all people; Leaders of Color often feel compelled to have an answer for everything; this is a recipe for disaster. Building strong relationships with students, faculty and staff, parents, and the school community will prove immeasurable in one's attempts to successfully lead a school.

In my experience, many district level leaders are satisfied with the status quo, and have little concern for improving the educational achievement of the children serve in marginalized communities.

3. Stand for Self-Care

Caring for oneself is the single most important thing a Leader of Color can do. A strong boy and mind permeates everything else a leader does to maintain and thrive in the uber-stressful position of school leadership. I suggest one be selfish with their time to reenergize. During my years as an educational leader, I have watched principals develop life-threatening physical conditions, deal with mental issues, divorce spouses, and become soured to the point that they were no longer effective leaders. Even I developed a stress-related health condition that slowed me down as a leader. It was at that point that I made radical changes to my life and work. I started by reevaluating my life and work and prioritizing them based on what was most important; what I found was that my job was nowhere near the top of my list! Being a school leader is what I do, not who I am.

Leaders of Color must be in the fight for the long haul, that means strengthening one's body and mind for longevity. Sports, exercise, fun activities are a must. Binge eating that comes with the job is unhealthy. I learned to schedule free time routinely—uninterrupted and unapologetically. Leaders must create scheduled times to cut off all things related to work, including e-mail, texts, and phone calls. To the chagrin of my supervisor, I stopped responding to middle-of-the-night e-mails and texts and informed her to stop disturbing me and my family with them. No, she did not like it but protecting my rest and off-duty time were important—and legal. Likewise, cutting off work and leaving the school building is a must. When I cut out long afterschool and weekend hours, my health improved. The reality is, that the long hours did not lesson the amount of work I needed to complete. We hurt ourselves with long work hours.

Learning to create margin in my life helped me to become better as a leader and as a family member at home. Having enough left over—emotionally, physically, financially, spiritually, provided me with the energy to give better and more of myself. Leaders, often working under duress and threat, tend to overextend themselves, and have no margin left in their lives. Learning to say no to after-hours work requests gave me the energy to become a stronger leader. As a practice, I do not contact my staff after hours or request anything of them during their off time. Love your students, love yourself, but love yourself and family more.

Professionally, one must build a cadre of trusted professional peers and mentors with whom ideas and opportunities can be shared. I made it a practice to form these relationships with people outside of my school district, primarily because many times I wanted to keep my future and personal development separate from my employment. I had worked with people who would sabotage and betray others, and I had had supervisors who tried to prevent my growth. I suggest diversifying one's professional development and taking every possible opportunity offered by the school district, but also looking outside.

CONCLUSION

Lastly, I strongly advise exploring and preparing for future employment opportunities. Leaders of Color must always be prepared for the next opportunity. Professional networking, researching, and publishing, and consulting provided me with opportunities I had not considered.

Leading a P–12 school is not for everyone; it takes a special skill set to be effective and progressive. Leaders of Color must know that they will be required to give more both personally and professionally. They will likely be assigned to the district's worst schools, with the fewest resources, and then threatened if they do not improve the school in an unreasonably short. The pressure faced by these leaders will be intense, but the rewards of success are incredible.

REFERENCES

Brooks, J. S., & Watson, T. N. (2018). School leadership and racism: An ecological perspective. *Urban Education, 54*(5), 631–655.

Echols, C. (2006). *Challenges facing Black American principal: A conversation about coping.* National Council of Professors of Education Administration.

Evans-Winters, V. (2016). Schooling at the liminal: Black girls and special education. *Wisconsin English Journal, 58*(2), 140–150.

Milligan, T., & Howley, C. (2015). Educational leadership in our peculiar institutions: Understandings of principals in segregated, White-staffed urban elementary schools in the United States. *International Journal of Multicultural Education, 17*(1), 43–49.

Patton, L., & Jordan, J. (2017). It's not about you, it's about us: A Black woman administrator's efforts to disrupt White fragility in an urban school. *Journal of Cases in Educational Leadership. 20*(1), 80–91.

CHAPTER 16

LEADING WHILE BLACK OR BROWN

Jerneé S. Kollock-Mann

I landed my first vice principal position in 2006, as a 31-year-old Black single mother, at a predominantly White suburban high school in southern New Jersey. It was my seventh interview, and I thought the interview would end up with a, "Thank you, but we will call you if anything opens up" To my surprise I was hired, and shortly after that, I would find out that I was the first African American woman hired as an administrator in that school district. The local newspaper even did an interview with me to highlight my recent appointment for the school district's most recent addition as a vice principal. I knew from that point this would be a position that would change my life professionally and personally as their first African American woman vice principal within this school district. There would be no school leadership program that could prepare me for what I was about to encounter for the next seven years of my tenure as a vice principal for this school district. I would definitely come to understand what it meant to lead while being Black or Brown in a predominantly White suburban school district.

I realized that accepting this job offer would mean that I would become a role model and mentor for students. I wanted to become a vice principal within a predominantly White school district. My reasoning for this

Purveyors of Change: School Leaders of Color Share Narratives of Student, School, and Community Success, pp. 139–147

strategic career move was because of what I experienced in my high school as a teenager. I wanted young teenage Black girls to see me every day, and to know that Black woman school administrators did exist. In addition, I wanted the White students to know that we existed as well. Most importantly, I was being a role model for my daughter.

WELCOME TO THE HECTIC WORLD
OF SCHOOL ADMINISTRATION

What I did not think about was the resistance that I would encounter from parents, administrative colleagues, and community members with embracing me as the new vice principal. I thought that I would receive automatic support from Black parents, but I was wrong. I remember a Black parent telling me that I was on the other side of the fence with the White people and not for Black people. That comment from the parent was the result of me having to suspend her daughter for cursing out a staff member and walking out of class without permission. I guess because her daughter shared the same skin color as me—that I overlook her rude and belligerent behavior. That parent's comment resonated with me and made me understand just how irrational people could be regardless of color. Another experience that resonated with me was a parent that I called back after hours. She called me earlier during the workday and I was unable to return her call during regular business hours, so I returned her phone call from my school issued cell phone, as I was leaving work at 4 P.M. During the conversation, she did not like the decision I made about her daughter, and she ranted that I was too young to even know about policy and procedures and had no business in the position as a vice principal. She called herself reminding me that I was in my position because my district needed to make a race quota, and this parent was White. That would not be the last time I would hear that I was hired because of race to meet the schools race quota.

I was then blind-sided by my principal informing me during my first couple of weeks on the job, my secretary that was assigned to me had some attendance issues, and that the office was a hot spot for students always wanting to visit her. So, if he knew this before I arrived why was not this issue addressed? Well, eight months into my job my secretary fell sick, and I found myself running the day-to-day operations within my office. It was stressful running my day-to-day operations of my office and carrying out my responsibilities as a new vice principal. Countless times, I approached my principal about finding me a replacement until my secretary came back, and I was turned down. My White female administrative colleague assigned in my school had two replacements for her previous secretary that year. All she did was asked once, and her requests were honored not once but twice. I would soon be a witness to how White privilege would play out in her favor, so that her office could operate successfully. Meanwhile, my office was being viewed as a spectacle, as I worked hard to turnaround the perception of how my office was operating. Being Black and female would be my motivation to work harder and have my office operate more efficiently for the sake of my students, staff, and parents.

It was always an uphill battle with having my voice heard about any issues concerning students, parents, or any pressing social issues that was impacting my school. There were countless times that my ideas were dismissed and just suppressed till they were silenced. I was constantly excluded from important meetings. This practice would infuriate me. I would only find out that I was excluded when a staff member would ask me the outcome of a particular situation, and I could not provide a response. After investigating, I would then find out that the reason I was unaware of outcomes was because my superiors and administrative colleagues excluded me from these types of meetings. It was very difficult for me to navigate the political hierarchical system that I worked for. I just tried my best to serve my students and provide teacher support in the best way that I could.

Every day for seven years I would come into that school and be constantly reminded about my race and gender. I did not realize how exhausting it was to lead as the only Black woman in my school, and in reality, I was the only Black female staff member in the school building. There were no other Black women that were teachers or staff members within my school building. I was the only Black female district wide for about two years. I felt isolated all the time and very alone on my own island.

WORK LIFE AND PERSONAL LIFE BALANCE

Being a vice principal was harder than what I perceived it to be when I was a teacher. There were times I would come home and just be so emotionally and physically exhausted. When the workday ended, I would come home and try giving my daughter a hundred percent with being a mother. I missed countless school activities for my daughter because I had to chaperone or attend work related activities. I tried to compromise by bringing her with me to work events when it was appropriate. At the time, my daughter was between the ages of 5–13, during my tenure as a vice principal. For me, it always hurt to see the sad look in her eyes whenever I arrived late to her games or was a no show to her events all because of my job. I had sacrificed so much for an organization that constantly disrespected me and isolated me.

CULTURAL SHOCK

It was a cultural and political shock for me working as a vice principal in this type of district. That is why I say that no graduate school could have prepared me for the obstacles that I encountered daily as a Black woman. I just learned to navigate the system and work around the challenges and address issues as I encountered them. There was a lot of bigotry and marginalizing with both students and staff members that stifled the school academically and culturally. Students of color were 10% of the population, and it was identified as a Title I school. That is because most of the student population parents were blue collar workers, held minimum wage jobs, and were not college educated. My secretary would give me a heads-up if parents were racist before I met with them, so I would know how to approach them. See, my secretary was born and raised in that town, so she grew up with most of the student's parents, so she understood the dynamics of the community. It was many times that I would overhear my secretary explaining to my White parents that I was not racist, that in fact their child's discipline was appropriately addressed by me. Having her in my office for that reason was a plus. It helped me to approach discussions with parents in a careful manner.

MY PERSONAL EXPERIENCE
WITH CULTURAL INSENSITIVITY

While I was a leader in this school I encountered my share of personal racial incidents. They were racial incidents that I should have reported to the central administration, but I always found myself addressing them with my building principal, and they would go undocumented. These were racial incidents I experienced from my own administrative colleagues. I was in my early thirties, and my confidence as a leader was still growing and maturing. I was not equipped with the emotional intelligence or self-awareness to engage with having these difficult conversations.

I became very interested in the lack of cultural competency within my school district. This prompted my central administrators to select me to oversee the districts diversity implementation initiative that was planned to address all dynamics of our school district, which ranged from increasing the numbers of students of color in Advance Placement classes to hiring more staff members of color. In addition, I was appointed affirmative action officer for my school district, district comprehensive equity officer, chair of diversity task force. I received a great deal of push back for overseeing this diversity implementation initiative. I was oblivious to the political circles and how they influenced my progress with implementing this diversity initiative. I would tiptoe around eggshells instead of just stepping on those eggshells. The resistance with my district to become culturally competent made me emotionally exhausted.

THE BEGINNING OF THE END

In March of 2012, I was asked to transfer to another sister high school on the other side of town, which was great for me for two reasons: (1) my commute was substantially shortened; (2) the student and parent population mirrored me professionally and culturally. I did not view the transfer as something negative, but something that could help catapult my career, and go onto become a district central administrator. In addition, my superintendent had already informed me that our sister high school needed a Black female, and he thought I would be the perfect candidate. Also, my principal assured me that this was a good career move for me to become a principal at that particular school, because becoming principal at my current high school would never happen. She stated that this high school's community members were not ready for a Black principal. To be honest, I did not even I want to be a principal not after what I was experiencing as a vice principal. I was unclear about the direction of my career path, and it was still up for debate if I even wanted to be in a K–12 setting as an administrator. Although, I was thriving in my career with holding various district level positions I was feeling unhappy and unfulfilled with creating real change with cultural awareness within my district.

In the Fall academic year of 2012, I had transferred to my new school, but it was not a smooth transition at all. I had become very overwhelmed with culturally insensitive remarks that were being made and circulating throughout the district. A district level supervisor within my building (White female) had told another district level supervisor (a White male) located in the school building where I was transferring that I was racist, did not know how to discipline, and I favored the Black students over the White students. The White male district supervisor at my soon to be new building assignment had told my new principal the gossip he received from the White female district supervisor at my old-school assignment. The principal at my newly assigned location decided to continue the gossip with the building secretaries. Someone close to me was loyal enough to inform me that they heard my principal talking about me in a negative way.

I decided to take a bold stand and inform my union president about the slander of my professional reputation that was occurring. My union president had gotten involved and brought these concerns to the district supervisors directly involved, as well as the principal. He would then schedule two separate meetings. The first meeting he held by himself was with my new principal. She confirmed that the district supervisors had told her the information about me. During their meeting, my principal would then offer to sit down with me and have an open and transparent discussion. I did agree to have a meeting with my new principal and my union president. My principal did indicate that she was upset because she was not made aware of my transfer until the board meeting. She had assumed that I had kept it from her, but I did not. I thought that certainly my superintendent had informed her before he even asked me about the transfer to her building. She apologized to me for slandering me professionally. The second meeting involved just my union president and the district supervisors. During this meeting, my union president threatened the district supervisors, that if it did not stop he was contacting the NAACP and getting them involved with this issue. I never met with them to discuss their professionally slandering gossip. They did not speak to me, and I did not speak to them It had gotten to the point where it became a hostile workplace environment for me. I could not understand why this was happening at the height of my career. I felt like my professional reputation was slowly slipping through my hands.

Unfortunately, in October 2012, my tenure was shortened due to being used as a scapegoat for my central administrators and three White female faculty staff members. Once again, I was excluded from a series of important meetings that landed me facing several criminal charges. My principal asked me to be a part of one meeting, in which she had already started an ongoing investigation pertaining to a student teacher relationship. I did not call the meeting or head up the investigation. Because I was 12th grade vice principal it was protocol for me to be a part of this meeting. Only if I would have been more politically aware of how this situation was unraveling- I could have saved my career and my personal life. This incident changed my professional and personal life forever. Seven years later my take on leadership is much different that it was 13 years ago—when I first became an administrator.

This life-changing incident, while tragic, proved to be the most important life lesson I could have been taught as a leader. I always thought of central administration as the support level for building administrators, and in addition they essentially were the ones to pick up the ball when it was dropped and made sure all of the I's were dotted and the T's were crossed. This situation taught me that just because someone is your subordinate does not mean that they are adequately and skillfully prepared to hold that esteemed leadership position. See, my central administrative team was made up of White men, and White privilege awarded them the opportunity to obtain their position—not their experience or hard work. My superintendent was only in his position for a year and half, and I witnessed how he allowed people to tell him how they would address issues. My principal was only in her position for about a year and a half as well, and she was always demonstrating a very laissez fair leadership style on a daily basis. So, I was not surprised that she found herself in a situation where she was convicted and lost her certifications.

As I read through my discovery evidence I saw how my principal was not provided any support and made decisions that should have been overseen by central administration. What I did not realize until I started reviewing documents of central administrators and my building principal was that—I was excluded from meetings that determined the outcome of the investigation. Being excluded from these meetings left me vulnerable when investigators wanted to speak to me about the incident. See, it was not unusual for me to meet with any type of law enforcement, so to me this was just a regular meeting to assist them with an investigation. Little did I know that I was the subject of their investigation. My immaturity as a leader left me vulnerable with not being able to read between the lines of what truly was about to turn my professional career upside down.

ADVOCATING FOR MYSELF

I remember the day I was contacted by superintendent that I had been placed on administrative leave. I asked my superintendent what was going on and he told me that he was asked not to discuss the situation with me, and that I had to leave the building. It was the coldest phone conversation I had ever had with him. I no longer could respect him, his central administration team, or my principal for placing me in a compromising situation. I refused to take any plea deal that the prosecutor's office offered, because I was not going to admit to something that was a lie just for the sake of this legal issue ending. The battle for advocating for myself started at that moment. It was imperative that I create my own social justice platform advocating for myself, because it was obvious no one was going to come to my defense.

For months and years, I would have to fight for my certifications and my professional reputation. I now knew what it meant to be a true leader who was Black. Forming and fighting on my own social justice platform would be a long arduous path for me. I would finally be cleared from any charges or lawsuits, but as I tried to apply for other vice principal positions I was essentially black balled. All school districts had to do was Google my name and they could come up multiple social media outlet reports about my school districts scandal that posted my picture and my name right at the forefront of their article. My case made national and internal headlines that would plague my professional career.

I was now experiencing leading from a different perspective that was new territory for me. I had to be able to stand up for myself and fight for what was right. The injustice I was experiencing throughout this entire ordeal was disheartening both professionally and personally. It did not matter that I was the administrator that led the plight with calls for reporting issues of child abuse or that I had lead an investigation two years previously that led to a coach being charged with endangering a child. My district's central administration team was not trying to be held accountable for conducting a sloppy investigation. It was obvious they were trying to save themselves from being charged or facing any criminal convictions. I read their interviews and witnessed how they lied about not knowing about the investigation. I thought to myself, "What type of leaders were they that possessed no integrity or ethics?"

My vice principal position gave me the opportunity to get some real skin in the game for being a leader. It is the best way I can describe my experience with being a vice principal within a predominantly White school district. The same unethical practices that hired me for this position would be the same unethical practices that would be the demise of my professional career. My experience allowed me to do some deep reflecting about the early years of my tenure as a vice principal, and how I would reinvent myself as an administrator without diminishing my core values and beliefs. It was imperative that if I was going to lead in any capacity that I had to be aware of political landscapes and the hierarchical decision makers. I had to develop the mentality that it was not personal it was s just business. I ultimately had to learn to advocate for myself, and not depend on anyone to advocate for me.

REBUILDING MY CAREER

My humility has sustained me with the energy and perseverance to rebuild my career. I realized that being a vice principal was not the only type of leadership position that I could possess. For years, I applied for vice principal positions and would feel so incomplete and dubbed myself as a failure when I was not selected for a vice-principal position. It was only through a deep sense of self-reflection that I realized I was limiting my potential as a leader by confining myself to the position as vice principal. My experience and credentials would be much more suited for providing support and creating conversations around the areas of teacher/administration professional developments and social justice issues pertaining to education.

Today, I lead different than I did 13 years ago. I am not fascinated with the leadership titles, but with leading to create a career path that pays tribute and homage to my ancestors that lost their lives to become educated; who wanted to attend college; who wanted to become educators. Throughout my seven years I have held several positions since resigning from my vice principal position-none of which were vice principal positions. Currently, I am a special education teacher within a psychiatric facility for 18–21-year olds. In addition, I have a registered educational consulting business where I contract various special educational services for various school districts. My career as a vice principal may have ended abruptly and caused me significant emotional distress, but I am still very passionate about the institution of education. Education is empowering and it is responsible for me sustaining resilience, perseverance, and grit for rebuilding my career. I was that high school sophomore told by her White male counselor that I would never get into a four-year college/university, but I did get accepted into a four-year historically Black college and university. Since I was a child I always loved education. My professional career in education is much bigger than being any school administrator.

Leading while Black has been an incredible and difficult journey. It has helped me to understand how important is to self-reflect and continue to grow as a leader in any facet for any job that I hold. I had to learn how to advocate for myself, which would allow me to advocate for others, and it is something that is ongoing for me. See, if I cannot be a strong advocate for myself, then how can I be strong enough to advocate for others. This is how I have learned to "Lead While Being Black or Brown."

ABOUT THE CONTRIBUTORS

EDITORS

Sheree N. Alexander currently serves as an adjunct professor in the Africana Studies Department at Rowan University and as a P–12 administrator for Atlantic City Public Schools. She holds an EdD in educational leadership, an MEd in school administration, and a BS in elementary education. Dr. Alexander has proudly served as a seventh and eighth grade language arts literacy teacher, assistant principal, instructional specialist, instructional support officer and professional development provider for the School District of Philadelphia, Academic Division 4. Dr. Alexander is interested in utilizing Restorative Practices in P–12 environments and creating trauma informed schools.

Judy A. Alston is professor and director of the Doctoral Program in Leadership Studies at Ashland University. She holds a PhD, a MDiv, two MEds, and a BA. She is the author of *Herstories: Leading with the Lessons of the Lives of Black Women Activists; Multi-leadership in Urban Schools;* and *School Leadership and Administration: Important Concepts, Case Studies, & Simulations.* Her research foci include Black female school superintendents; tempered radicals; refined revolutionaries; servant leadership; spirituality; and Black LGBT issues in leadership. Dr. Alston has been teaching for over 30 years.

Lawrence Scott currently serves as an assistant professor of educational leadership at Texas A&M University-San Antonio. Dr. Scott is also the executive director of the Community for Life Foundation, a scholarship fund that has given over half a million dollars to eligible students nationwide. Prior to higher education, Dr. Scott served 17 years in the P–12 sector as a secondary teacher, coach, guidance counselor, district-level curriculum specialist, and administrator in San Antonio ISD. Recipient of San Antonio Business Journal's 40 Under 40 "Man of the Year" in 2018, Dr. Scott is also known for his leadership and community outreach trainings at many universities, school districts, conferences, churches, and organizations such as the Federal Bureau of Investigation (FBI), Teach for America, Catholic charities, and even the NBA team San Antonio Spurs Sports and Entertainment. He lives in Texas with his wife Chiara and two children, Gabriella and Christian.

CONTRIBUTORS

Jamel Adkins-Sharif is a lecturer at Merrimack College and doctoral candidate in Urban Education Leadership and Policy at the University of Massachusetts-Boston. His research examines social justice leadership, race, and equity in schools. Jamel has had a successful career as a special education teacher in New York and was founding principal of an elementary charter and district middle school in Massachusetts. Additionally, Jamel served two terms on the principal's cabinet of the Massachusetts Department of Elementary and Secondary Education, and currently consults with the department on culturally proficient school improvement.

Willie Black, Jr. has had a successful career in K–12 public education, as a coach, teacher, principal, and director of human resources in the San Antonio Texas area. He has served as adjunct professor for the Department of Educational Leadership and Policy Studies at the University of Texas at San Antonio, and currently serves as an assistant professor and researcher at the University of Houston at Victoria. He has traveled around the country and spearheaded programs improving K–12 schools. As a public-school administrator Dr. Black supervised a diverse staff and student populations with a focus on social justice. Dr. Black has been in education for 22 years.

Joseph Cerna is a native of San Antonio, Texas. He earned his Bachelor of Sociology and Bachelor of Political Science degrees from the University of Texas at Austin, a master's degree in educational leadership and doctorate in educational leadership from the University of Texas at San Antonio. As a transformational leader in the public-school system for over 20 years, he has developed and presented sessions in the areas of at-risk, special education, English language learners, instructional technology, literacy, mathematics, educational leadership, and action research. Dr. Cerna is currently the principal of Fort Sam Houston Elementary and taught as an adjunct professor of educational research with Texas A&M University at San Antonio. His most recent research focuses on nontraditional forms of parental involvement.

Floyd Cobb has almost 20 years of experience spanning the P–20 educational continuum, holding roles as a teacher, school leader, district curriculum leader, and a statewide policy implementer. He holds a PhD in curriculum and instruction from the Morgridge College of Education at the University of Denver. There, he is an adjunct faculty member and teaches courses on social inequality through the lenses of race, class, and gender. In 2017, Floyd was awarded the Ruth Murray Underhill Teaching Award for excellence in teaching, which is given to one adjunct faculty member at the university. He has published numerous articles and book chapters and is the lead author of the book *Belonging Through a Culture of Dignity*, which focuses on dignity as a key component of equity implementation. He is also the author of *Leading While Black* (2017), an autoethnography detailing his reflections on the Black experience in educational leadership.

Raphael Crawford is a former Tennessee highly effective P–12 principal and district level administrator who currently serves as the chief consultant of the Crawford Group, LLC. He also serves as a principal mentor and as dean of instruction with Metropolitan Nashville Public Schools. He earned the EdD in leadership and the MEd in educational leadership from Trevecca Nazarene University. His research interests include the criminalization of Black boys, nontraditional families, mirror neurons, and ethical leadership, and urban school principals and superintendents.

Mateen A. Diop is an educator, author, publisher, and activist for the future of males of color. As an educator, Dr. Diop has served in every role and capacity in the K–12 arena. Beginning as a classroom teacher and leading district-wide departments and currently serving as the executive principal of Sam Houston High School and founding principal of Cyber P-Tech at Sam Houston High School. A staunch supporter of single-gender education, Dr. Diop is the founder of the newly created Young Men's Leadership Academy (YMLA) in the San Antonio Independent School District (SAISD). A first of its kind, the YMLA serves males in Grades 4–10, with the inaugural year (2015) opening with boys in Grades 4–6. This unique approach to serving young men was a concept Dr. Diop utilized while serving as the school principal at Herman Hirsch Elementary. "My dissertation research focused on single-gender education, and with hard data in hand, I knew the arrangement could be successful."

Donna Druery is currently a PhD candidate in educational administration at Texas A&M University, College Station, Texas. She holds a MA in leadership with a certification in school administration from Sam Houston State University in Huntsville, Texas. She has a BA in English from Texas A&M University. Donna also holds certifications in classroom teaching, college teaching, and superintendency. She has over 15 years of experience in public education. Her research foci include educational access and equity, charter schools and school choice, and tracking educational policies.

Renee L. Garraway received her doctorate from Bowie State University in the Culturally Responsive Educational Leaders in Special Education (CRELSE) cohort. She holds a master's degree in social work administration from The University of Michigan and a master's degree in special education from The George Washington University. Dr. Garraway has over 25 years of diverse work experience in clinical social work, special education, and school-based administration. She believes that her teaching, social work, and leadership experiences have provided fuel for her purpose and she is committed to ensuring that all students, regardless of race, socioeconomic status, or exceptional abilities receive rigorous, engaging and relevant instruction in a safe and nurturing learning environment.

Wil Greer is a father, husband, and educator. He completed his PhD in urban educational leadership from Claremont Graduate University in 2013. He joined Cal State University, San Bernardino in 2014 as a tenure-track assistant professor of educational leadership. Prior to becoming a professor Dr. Greer worked for 13 years in K–12 as a teacher and administrator. He has published nine studies, papers, and book chapters on the achievement and engagement of students of color. His current research interests include culturally responsive leadership, childhood trauma, and changing school culture.

Dorothy C. Handfield serves as the principal of alternative education and Newark Evening Educational Center—Newark Board of Education in Newark, New Jersey. Over the 22 years as an urban educator, she worked as an elementary school teacher, educational media specialist, vice principal, and principal. Dr. Handfield also has experience leading early childhood, elementary and high school buildings. She earned a Doctorate of Education from the University of Southern California, Masters of Arts degrees from Caldwell University and Kean University, and a Bachelor of Business Administration from Temple University. Dr. Handfield's areas of interest are traumatized children and/or youth and school discipline policies and practices.

Jerneé S. Kollock-Mann is currently a special education teacher for the Department of Health in New Jersey. She also works as a contracted special education home instructional tutor for various districts and is an adjunct professor for Widener University. Jerneé S. Mann is currently a doctoral candidate in educational leadership at Rowan University. Jerneé has had experience as a high school assistant principal, director of special education, and classroom teacher in public schools within rural, suburban, and inner-city school district settings. Jerneé S. Kollock-Mann has been in education for 23 years. Her previous experience in the position as an assistant principal prompted her to study Black women school leaders and intersectionality, and the ongoing workplace challenges she experienced as an assistant principal.

Cynthia Alexander Mitchell has served in public education for the past 23 years in various roles, ultimately serving in both school level and central office level administration for the 21st largest school district in the United States. Dr. Alexander Mitchell is also an adjunct professor teaching aspiring leaders pursuing their graduate degrees in Educational Leadership. She was also the formulary the president of the Memphis Public Schools Principal Association and was one of 30 Founding Principal/National Participants in the National Institute for Urban School Improvement leadscape, sponsored by the U.S. Department of Education. She has also served as a district, local, and national presenter. She holds an EdD, two MEds, and a BA Her research interest includes leadership development and identifying the primary tenets of culturally responsive urban school leaders.

Natalie D. Lewis is a middle school principal and a doctoral candidate in educational leadership and policy Studies at the University of Denver. Natalie began her educational journey as a guest teacher in the school district of Philadelphia. Since then she has had the opportunity of being a classroom teacher, a district support partner, assistant principal, and now principal in the Washington DC and Denver areas. Natalie's research centers on Black principals and family engagement.

Charisma S. Popillion is a high school principal in Beaumont, Texas who received her doctorate degree in curriculum and instruction from Texas Southern University in Houston, TX. As a former principal of an elementary school in Beaumont, Dr. Popillion successfully turned the school around within two years. She also holds MEd and BS degrees in educational leadership and interdisciplinary studies, respectively, from Lamar University in Beaumont, TX. Dr. Popillion has served in the field of education for a rewarding 17 years as a classroom teacher, curriculum coordinator, district-level supervisor, and the district coordinator for school improvement. She was also selected to participate in, through Raise Your Hand Texas, the 2019 Harvard Graduate School of Education: Art of Leadership Institute at Harvard University. She is the author of *An Examination of the Impact of School-Related Factors on the Reading and Mathematics Academic Achievement of Third Grade Hispanic Students*.

Lawrence Scott currently serves as an assistant professor of educational leadership at Texas A&M University-San Antonio. Dr. Scott is also the executive director of the Community for Life Foundation, a scholarship fund that has given over half a million dollars to eligible students nationwide. Prior to higher education, Dr. Scott served 17 years in the P–12 sector as a secondary teacher, coach, guidance counselor, district-level curriculum specialist, and administrator in San Antonio ISD. Recipient of San Antonio Business Journal's 40 Under 40 "Man of the Year" in 2018, Dr. Scott is also known for his leadership and community outreach trainings at many universities, school districts, conferences, churches, and organizations such as the Federal Bureau of Investigation (FBI), Teach for America, Catholic Charities, and even the NBA team San Antonio Spurs Sports and Entertainment. He lives in Texas with his wife Chiara and 2 children, Gabriella and Christian.

Patricia Virella serves as graduate faculty in the Art of Teaching Program at Sarah Lawrence College. She holds to MS Eds and a BS and is currently pursuing her PhD in educational leadership and policy at the University of Connecticut. Her scholarship focuses on education reform policy, principal preparation, and teacher education within the urban setting. Additionally, she is currently a Jackson Scholar.

C. Dedra Williams been an educator for over 25 years. After earning her GED and BA in language and literature, she continued graduate studies in Caribbean culture and society and achieved certifications in English as a second language and English as a foreign language, and then earned a master's degree in higher education and ultimately a doctorate in educational leadership. Various educational experiences, which extended from the United States to the Caribbean and Europe, enabled her to develop a worldview of culture and a multifaceted approach to life to understand needs of diverse learners. Dr. Williams specializes in English as a second language, English as a foreign language, teacher development, and diversity. She is a secondary educator and adjunct professor and was a school district administrator. Underserved learners, languages, and cultures and transformational progress remain the foundation of Dr. Williams's journey as an educator and lifelong learner.

Made in the USA
Middletown, DE
28 July 2021